Off the Record

BUZZIE BAVASI

with John Strege

CONTEMPORARY
BOOKS, INC.
CHICAGO • NEW YORK

Library of Congress Cataloging-in-Publication Data

Bavasi, Buzzie.
   Off the record.

   1. Bavasi, Buzzie.   2. Baseball—United States—
Managers—Biography.   I. Strege, John.   II. Title.
GV865.B33A3   1987   796.357'092'4 [B]   86-32942
ISBN 0-8092-4885-9

Dedication

To Evit, a member of my Hall of Fame for
more than 47 years.

Published by Contemporary Books, Inc.
180 North Michigan Avenue, Chicago, Illinois 60601
Manufactured in the United States of America
Library of Congress Catalog Card Number: 86-32942
International Standard Book Number: 0-8092-4885-9

Published simultaneously in Canada by Beaverbooks, Ltd.
195 Allstate Parkway, Valleywood Business Park
Markham, Ontario L3R 4T8 Canada

Contents

Foreword
By Reggie Jackson

It is only natural that Buzzie has written this book. He loves talking baseball. He particularly enjoyed talking about it with players who would take the time to stop by his office, which I frequently did. Most modern players don't do that anymore. No doubt it was one reason Mr. Bavasi decided to retire.

He preferred a family-type organization; a family-type situation similar to the one in which he worked for nearly thirty years with the Dodgers. He loves the sociology of the game as much as he loves the game itself.

However, the sociology has changed, just as the game itself has changed—to Buzzie's chagrin. He outgrew the sport and the sport outgrew him. He wanted the game to stay old-school, though I don't think he refused to change with it. He just didn't want to change his way of life. He dealt with us as if he were our uncle—our Uncle Buzzie. Buzzie wanted people to come to him with their problems and seek his help or advice.

A lot of players didn't like Buzzie because they thought he BS'd them a lot. One day, Buzzie was talking to me about my contract and the attendance clause included in it. He said that because the Angels held a lot of family nights and gave away a lot of tickets, those tickets should not be included in the clause. I said I didn't think that was right. "A deal is a deal," I said.

But he was serious about it. He talked with my attorney and my agent. Finally, I said, "Buzzie, you do whatever you want to do. I'll trust you to do what's right. Right now, I'm going down to the clubhouse to get ready for the game. Just let me know what you've decided as soon as possible."

When I got to the locker room, the phone was already ringing. It was Buzzie. He said, "You're right, Reggie, a deal is a deal." In the end, Buzzie was always fair.

The soaring salary structure bothered Buzzie. That didn't mean he minded paying stars big money. If they earned it, no problem. But he hated the idea that superstars—the million-dollar players—made it possible for $50,000 players to become $300,000 players. And he was right.

I don't think Buzzie's a business guy. I don't think he enjoyed that part of the game, although he was good at it. When we entered the era of million-dollar salaries, Buzzie went after the marquee stars. He knew with those players he had a good chance of winning. Equally important, he knew he was going to make money with them. Buzzie went for the double-agent type—guys who could do more than just play. He wanted players who could produce not only victories but revenue.

Buzzie is an old-schooler. He was born into, and

reared in, one of the best professional front offices in sports. You have the Boston Celtics, the Miami Dolphins, the Dallas Cowboys, the Los Angeles Raiders, the Baltimore Orioles, and the Dodgers, not necessarily in that order. Buzzie was taught under the tutelage of a very knowledgeable man, Branch Rickey. You can't do better than that.

To me, Buzzie is the kind of guy who was born at the age of 60 and will always be 60. He is always your dad, always your father. He has the jowls, the receding hairline, a heavyset way about him. I knew Buzzie when I was 19 years old. When I was 19 he looked 60. When I was 40, he still looked 60.

I regard it as a privilege to be considered one of his favorites. Here's a man who has seen millions of players, and he hand-picked a small group of guys he loved—Don Zimmer, Don Drysdale, Sandy Koufax, Roy Campanella, Don Newcombe, Pee Wee Reese, Steve Garvey, and Reggie Jackson.

If anyone can say they've seen it all, Buzzie can, and he tells it all here. I'm sure Buzzie has forgotten more about baseball than most general managers could hope to know.

He's still involved in the game, of course, always phoning players to advise them. He frequently offers advice to Angel vice president Mike Port and owner Gene Autry. But that's how it should be. When his time is up, he should die fooling around with baseball, just as I hope when Angel coach Jimmy Reese goes, it's on the field with a fungo bat in his hands.

I feel I could phone Buzzie any time, for any kind of advice. Or I could stop in and have lunch or dinner with him. I feel I could phone him to borrow twenty-five hundred dollars any time.

That's the way Uncle Buzzie is.

Acknowledgments

The authors wish to express their sincere thanks to all who participated in the histories and the stories contained within and to those who assisted in recalling them. Special thanks to Bob Hunter, Phil Collier, and John Hall, three of Southern California's finest sportswriters for more years than they care to remember, for their recollections and revelations.

We wish also to thank Larry LaRue for his advice and encouragement; Bob Mericle, for his computer assistance; Randy Youngman, for his manuscript assistance; and Shari Lesser Wenk, our patient, understanding, and talented editor at Contemporary Books, Inc.

Last, but certainly not least, we would like to thank Evit Bavasi and Marlene Strege, for their encouragement and assistance and for putting up with us.

1

Views and Overviews

From our home high on a hill overlooking the Pacific Ocean in La Jolla, California, my wife Evit and I have a panoramic view that is, in a word, breathtaking. It belongs on canvas and in a frame.

To expand the view, I have a powerful telescope that enables me to watch the kinds of stars that don't command millions of dollars for shining, or to watch the kinds of waves that haven't infested ballparks.

One day years ago, I discovered that with this telescope I could watch my son Bill's Little League baseball games six miles away. One particular afternoon, he struck out and threw his helmet, a scene to which I was a witness courtesy of the telescope. At dinner that night, I asked, "Son, what happened today?"

"I struck out," Bill said.

"No, I don't mean that. Why'd you throw your helmet?"

He was incredulous. He knew I wasn't at the game,

yet I had seen him throw his helmet. The lesson here is that you need not be at the game to see what is happening.

To see what is happening in the game today, you need only to read the sports section of the newspaper. The box scores are inside. On page one are too many stories of greedy athletes and agents, of strikes not called by umpires, of a game gone awry. Times have changed, and not necessarily for the better. Of this, I was a witness up close.

The view from my office was much the same as the view from my home. It was unobstructed and tele-scopical. For more than four decades, I was permit-ted to sit in the upper echelons of baseball manage-ment, where I watched the game evolve from something I love into something I don't entirely understand.

From where I sit today, I can look at the past and see a lifetime of pleasant memories, a few unpleasant ones, and little that I would change given the chance. I can look at the present and see too much I would change. I see businessmen in knickers hoping to get rich quick from a game that was meant to be played for fun. I see agents taking millions of dollars out of the game and never putting a dime back into it.

Consider, for a moment, what baseball does for agents. The average salary of a major league player on opening day of 1986 was $431,521. The total payroll was $283,941,298. If the agents' average com-mission was five percent, the agents, then, would have taken $14.2 million out of baseball in 1986. If their average commission was just three percent, they still would have taken $8.5 million out of the game. Now, consider what agents put back into baseball and you see the problem.

Arbitration is another disturbing by-product of the modern game. One year, we lost an arbitration hearing on an outfielder, Bobby Clark, who batted .211. We had a pitcher, Dave Frost, who won four and lost eight, and the arbitrator ruled in his favor, giving him a raise. Yet another time, we had the arbitrator ask us before a hearing began, "What's an ERA?" We knew we were in trouble.

I was in baseball for 45 years and I never had an ulcer, because I enjoyed what I was doing. Then, when I was out of the game for a year, I was hospitalized with a bleeding ulcer. I pick up the paper and see what is happening with this game and I get sick.

To illustrate one way the game has changed in the last 45 years for better or for worse, consider a first baseman we had at Valdosta, Georgia, in 1942, John Hernandez, the father of Keith Hernandez. John Hernandez was making $125 a month for four months. That's $500 for the year. Keith makes that in one inning today.

I don't begrudge the quality players their money. They deserve it—a Reggie Jackson, a Doug DeCinces. It's the 23rd and 24th players on a club, getting $300,000 or more, who don't deserve it.

In fact, the 1985 California Angels had 11 players who each made more than the entire 1955 Brooklyn Dodger team: Rod Carew, Bobby Grich, Bob Boone, Doug DeCinces, Brian Downing, Reggie Jackson, Geoff Zahn, Ken Forsch, Mike Witt, Rick Burleson, and Tommy John.

When I look back at that 1955 Dodger team, I think about how much you'd have to pay those guys if they were in their primes today. Duke Snider, Gil Hodges, Roy Campanella, Carl Furillo, Pee Wee Reese, Jackie Robinson, Carl Erskine, Don Newcombe. One organization could not afford them all at once.

In 1986, the minimum major league salary was $60,000. Campanella never made more than $36,000,

Robinson $39,000, Hodges $40,000, Snider $38,000.

Whatever my disillusionment with the game today, it cannot detract from the enjoyment I've derived from baseball. I've been very fortunate in this game. Lou Gehrig said once, "I'm the luckiest man in the world." He has company—I think I'm the luckiest man in the world. I have a wonderful wife and four of the finest sons for whom anyone could wish. I can't ask for anything more.

Never before in the history of baseball had a father and son operated major league baseball clubs at the same time until Peter, our oldest son, created and operated the Toronto Blue Jays in the 1970s, when I was operating the San Diego Padres.

Our youngest son, Bill, is the director of minor league operations for the California Angels, and doing a fine job. Chris, our second son and the only one not involved in baseball, has a most responsible and rewarding position as executive director of a federal Indian program. He is also a city councilman in Flagstaff, Arizona.

Alaska Airlines Magazine wrote a story about our third son, Bob, entitled, "All-American Couple Lives the All-American Dream." He and his wife, Margaret, both attorneys by trade, left their law careers and purchased the Walla Walla, Washington, franchise of the Northwest League, and moved it to Everett, Washington. Today, the Everett Giants are flourishing, boosted by a working agreement with the San Francisco Giants.

To me, baseball is still more enjoyable at the minor league level. I envy Bob right now; he's having a ball. Evit and I had a wonderful time in the minor leagues, where you can be your own boss. When I was at Valdosta, or Americus, Georgia, nobody would tell me what to do, if only because nobody cared to come down to Valdosta or Americus to tell me what to do.

The pictures on the walls of my den serve as reminders of happier days in baseball. Today's game is represented by a single photo, of Reggie Jackson and Steve Garvey. It is obvious I'm more fond of the past than the present. I look at these pictures and ask myself what other man can claim as friends American League president Bobby Brown; former commissioner Bowie Kuhn; Gene Autry; Chub Feeney; Horace Stoneham; and Lee MacPhail, among a long list of others.

I am an ordinary man from Scarsdale, New York, who has had the privilege to sit at World Series games with General Douglas MacArthur and President Eisenhower, to sit with President Nixon at Angels games, to know presidents Ford and Reagan. Baseball gave me these opportunities.

When I was just out of college, I was lucky to get a job in baseball, and a few years later I found myself having breakfast with Carl Hubbell and Mel Ott and having dinner with Bill Terry, all of them boyhood idols of mine and now Hall of Famers.

I have been fortunate to work for people who were experts in their fields. Larry MacPhail, my first employer in baseball, was the greatest promoter in the game, Bill Veeck notwithstanding. Branch Rickey was the greatest judge of talent the game has ever known. Walter O'Malley knew the business aspect of the game better than anyone. The late Ray Kroc, who owned the San Diego Padres and was the McDonald's hamburger magnate, was an extraordinary salesman, one who could sell baseball as well as he sold hamburgers. Last, but certainly not least, was Gene Autry, who is a composite of all of them. Autry, too, is a great baseball fan.

The thing for which I'm most proud, if I have the

right to be proud of anything, is that so many people who worked for me became major league managers. Among them were Walter Alston, Tommy Lasorda, Gene Mauch, Dick Williams, Sparky Anderson, Danny Ozark, Don Zimmer, Doug Rader, Joe Altobelli, Bob Lillis, Larry Shepard, Frank Howard, Bobby Valentine, Gene Michael, Clyde King, Roy Hartsfield, Jeff Torborg, John Goryl, Billy Hunter, Bob Kennedy, Lefty Phillips, Frank Lucchesi, Preston Gomez, and Rene Lachemann, who started as a Dodger batboy.

My greatest thrill in baseball these days is seeing men who once played for me now entering the Hall of Fame. There are so many of them now: Koufax, Drysdale, Campanella, Snider, Reese, Robinson, and, of course, the man who managed them, Walter Alston. And in the future, Don Sutton, Rod Carew, and Reggie Jackson will join them.

These were the kind of men who deprived me, not unhappily, of a summer vacation. In 45 years in baseball, I never had a summer vacation—instead, I had a summer vocation. For me, it was much the same. Others would spend their vacations in parks, but I spent my vocation in parks, too, from Ebbets Field in Brooklyn to the Coliseum and Dodger Stadium in Los Angeles to Jack Murphy Stadium in San Diego and finally to Anaheim Stadium.

It was a 45-year journey through two distinct eras of our national pastime. My career began when the game was lily-white, the color of innocence. The people who ran it then were guilty only of poor judgment, for taking so long to racially integrate the game.

My career ended after the 1984 season, when baseball no longer had a claim on innocence of any kind. It had become a business first, a game second, and drugs and greed had begun to surface.

From beginning to end, I was a participant of and

a witness to baseball history and history makers. I
was fortunate to be given a minor role in Jackie
Robinson's breaking through the major-league baseball color barrier, in 1947.

As the executive vice president of the Dodgers, I
saw hearts broken in 1951 and mended in 1955, at
what were arguably the lowest and highest points in
Dodger history. The club lost a 13½-game lead and
the National League pennant to its arch rival, the
New York Giants, in 1951, in what was called the
Miracle at Coogan's Bluff. In 1955, the Dodgers won
their first World Series, beating the Yankees in seven
games.

I was involved in the club's move from Brooklyn to
Los Angeles in 1958, which officially began the era of
the jet set in baseball. We missed the trains then, and
I still miss them now.

I saw Dodger Stadium built from scratch on what
by now is some of the most expensive real estate in
the nation. Unbeknownst to many, Chavez Ravine
had not been the only site under consideration; Walter O'Malley had looked at property in Inglewood,
too. The biggest drawback at the Inglewood site was
that it sat across the street from a cemetery. Having
just moved from one graveyard, dilapidated Ebbets
Field in Brooklyn, the Dodgers weren't about to move
to another.

Later, as an executive vice president of the Angels,
I played a significant role in signing Reggie Jackson,
one of baseball's most colorful and controversial
characters ever.

My career, then, spanned roughly from Robinson
to Reggie. Not surprisingly, I prefer the game of
Robinson's era to the way it is in Reggie's era. And I
wouldn't give up the early days in Brooklyn for all of
the last 30 years.

As for that ocean view at my home, Yogi Berra once

looked out the window and, startled, asked, "What the hell's all that water doing out there?"

"What do you mean," I said, like others, not quite sure what Yogi was talking about.

"What is it?"

"It's the Pacific Ocean, what the hell do you think it is?"

"Oh."

2

God Bless Americus: The Beginning

First, let me explain the origin of my name. My given name is Emil, but as a young boy I was, in a sister's words, "Always buzzing around." She began calling me Buzzie, and it stuck.

My mother probably wanted to call me many things when she discovered I was not where I was supposed to have been for four years. I was supposed to have been attending DePaul University in Chicago. My mother had wanted me to attend a "good Catholic school."

In fact, I was attending DePauw, a good Methodist school in Indiana. All my bills went straight to the family lawyer, so for four years, my mother thought I was attending DePaul. She did not find out otherwise until she attended my graduation in 1938. Fortunately, she did not hold it against me. She still presented me with a marvelous graduation gift: time. She gave me a year off to do whatever I wished to do, before I'd be required to enter the real world.

At the time, she had a house in Clearwater, Florida, where the Dodgers then trained. All I wanted to do was to go to Clearwater during spring training in 1939 and watch the Dodgers train.

In March of 1939, I was watching a game in Clearwater, and Ford Frick, then the president of the National League, was there, too. I had known Mr. Frick since my dad died in 1933. Mr. Frick's son Fred and I had roomed together at DePauw (and we've remained friends for 50 years).

"What are you doing here?" Mr. Frick asked me.

I explained that my mother had given me the year off. "And I've got two more months to go," I said.

"No you haven't. Be in my office tomorrow."

"What office?"

"In New York."

I flew to New York, where Mr. Frick took me by the hand to see Larry MacPhail, then the president of the Brooklyn Dodgers. Ford asked Larry to give me a job, and he did, as a glorified office boy. I didn't get paid for 13 weeks.

I enjoyed the office work, doing odds and ends and helping Branch Rickey, Jr., the Dodgers' farm director. He once invited me to sit in on a meeting with him, Harold Roettger, and several scouts. They were going through a list of prospects when they came across a right-handed pitcher whose name I recognized.

One of the scouts mentioned that this pitcher had pitched at Purdue. I had played against him while I was attending DePauw. Nevertheless, I kept my mouth shut for the time being. That night, I got out my scrapbook and looked up the box score of that Purdue game. It was indeed the same pitcher. DePauw had won the game and I had gotten three hits. So I took the box score into the office the next day.

Larry MacPhail was prepared to pay this pitcher a

bonus of $1,500. Then he read the box score and tore
the contract up. Larry turned to me and said, "If you
can get three hits off him, we don't want him." And to
this day, I feel guilty. The fellow might have been
another Dizzy Dean. Who knows?

In January of 1940, the Dodgers needed a business
manager for their Americus (Georgia) Pioneers
team, in the Class D Georgia-Florida League. I applied, and MacPhail gave me the job.

A banner headline in the newspaper there, the
Americus Pioneer, announced my arrival:

BAVASI ARRIVES TODAY

Nearly 40 years later, I recalled this headline after
reading a story with an Americus dateline in the *Los
Angeles Times*. The story told of President Carter's
visit to Americus, a town about nine miles from his
hometown of Plains. This story, however, carried a
rather small headline.

President Carter's national chairman, Bob
Strauss, is a friend of mine, and I told him about the
headline I got when I went to Americus, comparing it
with the size of the headline President Carter com-
manded. Bob suggested I send the clippings to the
president, that he'd get a big kick out of them.

So I did. I enclosed a note saying, "Dear Mr.
President, Things have changed. When I arrived in
Americus, I got a much larger headline than you did
when you arrived there."

A short time later, much to my surprise, I received
a handwritten note from the president. "Yes, I re
member you well," President Carter wrote. "My
uncle was on your board of directors."

Although the name meant nothing to me at the
time, a Carter had indeed been on my board of
directors in Americus. In retrospect, it was appropri-

ate; I was working for peanuts. I was making perhaps $120 a month.

Nevertheless, I was a big wheel in Americus. I
organized the club quickly, and with some leisure
time on my hands, I decided Evit and I should get
married in Americus, rather than having the wedding back home in Scarsdale after the season. I
persuaded Evit and both our families to come to
Georgia.

I met my mother and sister at the train station, and
that evening I received a lunch invitation from Jim
Blair, the editor and publisher of the *Americus
Pioneer*.

"Buzzie, you can't do this to us," he said at lunch the
next day. "You've been in Americus about two
months and people have taken you to heart. They like
the way you do business, and they've made you one of
our own. But Judge Smythe is furious."

"What are you talking about?" I asked.

"The judge's secretary was at the train station
yesterday, when your good bride got off the train.
And she has to be 7½ months pregnant. And this is
why you're getting married down here instead of at
home."

I laughed. "That wasn't Evit," I said. "That was my
sister, who is 7½ months pregnant."

To this day, I never got word to the judge, who had
been invited to the wedding. He did not show up.

Like I was, Evit was raised in Scarsdale. I first saw
her when I was 13½ and she was 12 and she was doing
a Scottish dance, the Highland Fling. I said to myself, "Gee, she's cute. I'm going to marry that girl."
Ten years later, we were married.

But first, I needed a best man. The Pioneer
player-manager, Bernie deViveiros, was the only
Catholic on the club, so he was elected by default.

Then we needed a Catholic church. Americus had none, so we went to Albany. The wedding was at 11 A.M., and we had a ball game four hours later and 60 miles away.

After the reception, Evit and I drove to the game. When it started, the Pioneers were without their manager. DeViveiros was sitting in the stands.

"Bernie, what are you doing up here?" I asked.

"Well, I had some champagne at the reception," he said, "and when I went to give the batting order to the umpire, I told the big SOB, 'If you're going to throw me out, throw me out now.' And he did."

Everything was great for a few weeks, until Larry MacPhail called to tell me he was sending Stew Hofferth, a catcher, to Americus.

"We don't need a catcher," I said. "We've got a great young prospect here by the name of Danny Twitchell."

"Catcher? Stew's not coming in to catch. He's coming in to manage."

"To manage?" I said. "What do I do with Bernie?"

"Fire him."

"But, Mr. MacPhail, I can't do that. He was the best man in my wedding."

"Fire him anyway."

This was my initiation into the often heartless world of professional baseball. The night I was supposed to fire him, deViveiros put himself in to pinch hit in the ninth inning of a tie game, with a man on first and two outs. He tripled, and we won the game. Although I'd made up my mind to fire him, I simply couldn't do it then.

The next morning, I read in *The Sporting News* that the Meridian, Mississippi, club was looking for a manager, and it was willing to pay $350 a month. Bernie was making $300 with us. I called Meridian on Bernie's behalf and accepted the job for him. Then I explained to Bernie the favor I had just done for him.

"Bernie, I just accepted another offer for you, to manage Meridian," I said. "You've got to take this job. It means $50 a month more for your family. Fifty dollars a month for four months is $200. You'd better take it."

He agreed, and the very next day, Bernie left for Meridian.

My professional playing career began and ended in Americus, and consisted of three games, 12 at-bats, four hits, and an unpromising inning on the mound. At the end of the season, MacPhail had called me and asked that I send three players to our Dayton club, which was in the playoffs.

"But that would leave me with only eight players," I told him.

"That's too bad. I don't know what you're going to do."

We had three games left, a single game and a doubleheader against George Sisler, Jr.'s Albany team. At DePauw, I had been a pretty good catcher. I had batted .450 and was offered $1,500 by Bill Terry to play for a club in Tennessee. But I was slow and I didn't think I had major league ability. So instead of signing, I went fishing with my mother.

But now, I had no alternative. I would play professionally after all, if only for a weekend. I opened the first game at second base for Americus. By the eighth inning, our pitcher had tired and I relieved him. The first man I faced hit a home run, and *his* teammates came to the mound to congratulate me— it was the first home run the kid had hit in his four years in professional baseball.

In 1941, we had moved the Americus club to Valdosta. Stew Hofferth, our player-manager, was batting .365, and we were leading the league by 10 games when Larry MacPhail called again.

"I'm sending Bud Clancy down," he said. At the time, Bud was managing and playing first base at Santa Barbara.

"Mr. MacPhail, we don't need a first baseman. We've got John Hernandez playing first."

"He's not coming in to play first, he's coming in to manage."

"Mr. MacPhail, Stew's hitting .365 and we're leading the league by 10 games."

"I don't care what he's doing. Get rid of him."

Instead of simply firing Stew, we sent him to Brooklyn, where the Dodgers gave him a train ticket to Toronto. Larry's son, Lee MacPhail, who would later become president of the American League, was the general manager of the Toronto club in the International League.

Lee signed Stew to a Toronto contract for $300 a month legally and $300 a month under the table. In those days, the salary limit in the International League was $12,000 a month per club; had he given Stew all $600 a month above board, the club would have exceeded the limit and been subject to a fine.

As it was, baseball commissioner Judge Kenesaw Mountain Landis discovered what had been done and summoned Stew and me to his office in Chicago. When I arrived, Stew was already in the judge's office. About two hours later, they emerged, and the commissioner, with his arm around Stew, said to me, "We don't need you, young man. I just made him a free agent."

The commissioner thought he was doing Stew a favor by giving him his free agency. In fact, the commissioner had done him a disservice. Stew had had a job making $600 a month and he was happy. Now he was unemployed.

He returned to his home in Gary, Indiana, out of a

job, and I went with him. We decided to have a few drinks, since he was interested only in drowning his sorrows. I had had about one too many myself when I decided to call Donie Bush, the owner of the Indianapolis club. Bush was a good friend of Ted McGrew, who was employed by the Dodgers. I asked Donie if he needed a catcher who had hit .365 at Valdosta.

"No, I don't think so," Bush said.

I must have had another drink, because by then I was full of courage. I called Ted McGrew and said, "Ted, this guy can do it all, can you help us out? Can you try to get him a job with Indianapolis?"

"I'll call you back," Ted said.

He called back about midnight. "All right, fine, he's got a job."

"How much?" I asked.

"What do you mean how much?"

"We want $900 a month," I said boldly, through the blur of the evening's libations.

He called back an hour later and said $900 was agreeable.

"Wait a minute," I said, my confidence further bolstered. "The $900 is fine, but we've got three other clubs that want this fellow. We want a bonus."

"What do you mean a bonus?"

"We want a bonus."

Ted called back at 2:30 A.M. and said, "You dumb son of a bitch. Donie's going to give you the bonus."

That was my first inkling of what it was like to be an agent. You had to be bold, abrasive, and able to skirt the truth.

A footnote: Indianapolis later sold Stew to the Boston Braves for $19,500, so the club actually made money on him.

The same year, the Dodgers purchased the Reading, Pennsylvania, club. For $5,000, they received a bus, a set of uniforms, and 12 players, one of whom was Carl Furillo.

Lee MacPhail was named the general manger of the new club and Fresco Thompson was his manager. One day, when Fresco was coaching third base, a woman in the stands was giving him hell for the way he wore his pants. He had pants like Carl Hubbell— the pant legs went down to the tops of his shoes.

After a few innings of abuse, Fresco had heard enough, and he went over and said to the woman, "Why don't you lay off me? This is the way I like my pants. They're comfortable."

"She's got a right to say anything she wants about your pants," the woman's husband interjected.

"Well, I'll say one thing for my pants," a miffed Fresco replied. "They're a lot better than the ones she forgot to put on."

The lady, wearing a skirt, was without an important part of her wardrobe.

The first time I encountered Commissioner Landis was a memorable experience for me. I had been invited to the 1940 World Series in Cincinnati by Ford Frick. We were in the lobby of the hotel when Judge Landis arrived and discovered that a suite had not been reserved for him. He engaged in a heated argument with the hotel clerk, who attempted to explain why the commissioner was without a suite.

Finally, Judge Landis had had enough. Poking the clerk in the chest, the commissioner said, "Young man, what you're doing is called, in the hotel business, 'giving me the run-around.' In baseball, we call it 'bullshit.' "

When the matter was resolved, we went up to Mr. Frick's suite to have a drink, and the conversation turned to Judge Landis's favorite subject, Leo Durocher.

"Let me tell you about that Presbyterian son of a bitch," the Judge said. Landis called everyone a Presbyterian son of a bitch. "Years ago, he wrote a check, but didn't have enough money in the bank to cover it. I called him into my office and told him if he ever made out a check again as long as he was in baseball, I'd ban him for life.

"Now months later, his first wife came in to see me. She was complaining that Leo hadn't paid her any alimony or child support for six months. So I called Leo in and said, 'Leo, if you don't pay your wife the alimony, I'm going to ban you from baseball.' "

"And Leo says, 'Judge, you told me not to write any more checks. So I didn't.' "

Larry MacPhail was another volatile character. Working for him wasn't always profitable for me. He would make me go to the race track with him, and invariably I'd lose part or all of what I was paid each week.

I remember Larry asking a handyman employed by the club, Babe Hamburger, to go down to the bank and bring back "four hundred-dollar bills," so he could go to the track. Babe returned instead with 400 dollar bills, which Larry proceeded to throw across the room, money flying everywhere.

The year 1943 was the worst of our lives. We went to Durham, North Carolina, where the Dodgers had a Class B club in the Piedmont League. The club was basically pathetic. Every time we'd get a player with ability, he'd be promoted. Gene Mauch played on that team; so did Rex Barney and Gene Hermanski and all were sent to a higher classification club during the season.

One day, Branch Rickey, who became president of the Dodgers that year, sent me a shortstop, Gene Moore, whom the Durham newspaper proclaimed was the "new Durocher." This was the first of too

many errors we would see in the next week: in his
first six games, Moore averaged about three errors a
game.

Mr. Rickey suggested that he had erred in signing
the boy, that Moore's hands were too small. When
Moore's father read what Mr. Rickey had said, he
came into my office more than a little irate.

"Mr. Rickey ruined my boy's career," Mr. Moore
said. "We want our release."

By now I thought I knew Mr. Rickey pretty well.
He wouldn't give anybody his release, especially
when he had bestowed a bonus upon a player. To sign
Moore, he had given him $3,600. I called Mr. Rickey
and explained the dilemma.

"Well, he can't play," Mr. Rickey said. "See if you
can get him to give us $1,800 back."

I explained to Moore and his father that we
couldn't simply release the boy after giving him
$3,600. "I just don't think it's right for me to waste
Mr. Rickey's money," I said.

Moore's father pulled out his checkbook. He was
going to refund us the entire $3,600. Then my eyes lit
up. I could picture Mr. Rickey giving me $1,800 for a
job well done.

"Wait a minute," I said to Mr. Moore. "You're
forgetting one thing. We gave the boy $300 in salary."

Mr. Moore gave me a check for $3,900. But I guess
I did not know Mr. Rickey as well as I thought I did.
Not only did I not receive a nickel for my diligence, I
did not receive so much as a thank-you for saving him
$2,100 above what he had expected.

It seemed that every day brought a new problem.
We had a little left-handed pitcher, who, it seemed,
was spending too much time with a lady of question-
able character. We thought she was a groupie, to
borrow a phrase from the eighties.

We were playing a game in Roanoke, Virginia, when I walked through the lobby of our hotel, spotted this girl, and thought to myself, "Oh, no, we can't have this. These are young boys here. We can't have girls following the club."

So I called our manager, a feisty little man named Bruno Betzel, and told him about it. He called the player, told him to come to a meeting in his room, and to bring the girl. I was there, too.

"Damn you," Bruno said to him. "I'll fine you every dime you've got if you ever do this again. I don't want any damn broad of her kind following us around."

Bruno turned to the girl and said, "And you, you get your ass out of here."

With that, the player handed Bruno a piece of paper. It was a marriage license. They had been married the night before.

I didn't know what to do. Bruno had just called this guy's wife a "broad" in tones that suggested she was something worse. I had $30 in my pocket that I gave the couple and told them to go out and have a good time. I didn't know what else to do.

The following day, the player came in to see me and asked to buy out his contract. "Buzzie, I'm really embarrassed," he said. "I can't stay."

I called Mr. Rickey, who suggested I sell the boy his contract for $12,000. The player agreed to buy it.

"Here," he said, handing me a $20 bill. "Put it on my account. I'll pay the rest when I get it."

He had $20 to his name and he was going to buy out his contract for $12,000.

We always needed pitching that year, one time so much so that I went on radio and made a public plea. "If anybody listening can pitch," I said, "please come on into Durham. You might have a job."

The next day, this great big young pitcher arrived,

Pat Patterson, about 6'5" and 240 pounds. I asked him whether he had any experience.

"Yeah," he said.

"Where'd you pitch?"

"Atlanta."

Atlanta was in a Class AA league then. Durham was in only a B league. "I've got something here," I said to myself.

A few days later, Patterson pitched both ends of a doubleheader, winning the first game, 1-0, and losing the second game, 2-1. I was impressed. He won three of his first five decisions. Then, like so many before him, he left us, but this time, it wasn't the Dodgers who took him.

I was sitting in my office when one of our outfielders, Walter Chipple, came to see me. He was white as a sheet.

"Five of us were playing poker in my room," he explained, "when the door was broken down. Three men with guns drawn came in and took Patterson away. They said they were with the FBI."

I called the FBI office and, sure enough, they had arrested Patterson. He was, as I understood it, a draft dodger. But he wasn't lying about having played at Atlanta. He was talking about the Atlanta penitentiary.

Rex Barney pitched for us at Durham, only to have the Dodgers summon him to Brooklyn. Late in the season, Mr. Rickey had sent me a wire requesting me to "Send Barney to Brooklyn immediately."

When I received the telegram, we were in the sixth inning of a game in Lynchburg, Virginia, ahead, 2-0, and Barney was pitching. I showed the wire to Bruno, who in turn showed it to Barney. He told Rex that if he could end the game quickly, he could make an 11 o'clock train to New York.

Barney had an exceptionally strong arm, like No-

lan Ryan. Barney struck out seven of the last nine
batters and made his train easily.

World War II beckoned in 1943. A father with an
infant son, Peter, I expected to miss out on the
experience of wearing a uniform that didn't have a
number on the back. I had been offered a commission
as a junior-grade lieutenant, but declined on the
grounds that I had a family to support.

Two weeks later, my draft status changed to 1-A. I
went to Grand Central Station for a physical, entered
the U.S. Army, and served three years as a machine-
gunner in Africa and Italy. Whereas in my civilian
days I wouldn't walk across the street to get a
newspaper, in the war I walked from Naples all the
way to the Austrian border.

When I was discharged in 1946, Mr. Rickey named
me the business manager of the Dodgers Class B
farm club in Nashua, New Hampshire, where I first
encountered a man who would enrich all our lives
over the next 30 years. His name was Walter Alston.

Walter was the manager at Nashua. He made only
one mistake that year, this one off the field. And it
could have dramatically altered his career.

Alston, Larry Shepard (later the manager of the
Pittsburgh Pirates), Dick Malady, and I were playing golf one day, and I made a hole-in-one. In those
days, you received a case of whiskey, tires for your
car, and other assorted gifts for a hole-in-one. They
were rare then, because so few people played golf.
Afterward, the three refused to sign my scorecard, a
necessary action to make the ace official.

"Fine," I said. I called Evit and asked her to pull
three release forms out of my desk and to bring them
to me. I actually filled them out, handed one to each
of them, and said that unless they signed my card,
they were through.

Eventually, they signed. I've always said that if

Walter hadn't signed that scorecard, no one would ever have heard of him. Was I kidding? He'll never know.

Before the 1946 season, I received a call from Mr. Rickey regarding a decision that was instrumental in changing the face of baseball. Mr. Rickey said that his assistant, Bob Finch, was coming to Nashua to see me on an important matter that was to be kept a secret. He told me to arrange a meeting and to have the club president in attendance.

We held the clandestine meeting at midnight, and Finch disclosed that Mr. Rickey wanted the Nashua club to take two players, Roy Campanella and Don Newcombe.

"What's the secret?" I asked, wondering why we were assembled after midnight to discuss Nashua's roster.

"He offered them to the Danville club in Illinois," Finch said. "The club didn't think they should take them."

"What do you mean, 'Take them?' " I asked.

"Well, they happen to be black."

"Can I go 10 miles from here and find two players as good as they are?" I asked

"No," Finch replied.

"Then I want them." I couldn't have cared less as long as they could play. It made no difference to me.

At the same time Jackie Robinson was breaking the color barrier in the International League, Campanella and Newcombe were breaking it in the New England League.

The people in Nashua loved these two. Walter had so much faith in Campanella, in fact, that on the rare occasion that Alston was ejected from a game, he'd put Campy in charge. To this day, I think Campy would have made a fine manager.

Racial incidents were minimal. The diminutive

manager of the Lynn, Massachusetts, club, Pip Kennedy, verbally abused Campy and Newk throughout one game, hurling racial slurs nonstop for nine innings. Campy and Newk never batted an eye, they never complained.

After that game, when the home team would provide the visiting club with its share of the gate, I purposely made Kennedy wait. Finally, he got obnoxious about it, advising me in angry tones to hurry up. Evit and Mrs. Alston were present, too, waiting for Walter and me.

I got up and said to this manager, "Don't you talk that way in front of my wife and Mrs. Alston or I'll knock you on your fanny. Come on outside."

I was going to belt him, knowing, of course, that Alston was right behind me. (Just to make sure, though, I kept turning around to check.) Alston could take on a whole ball club, he was that kind of a man. I told Kennedy that if he ever called Campy and Newcombe niggers again I'd kill him. We had no more trouble with Pip Kennedy.

Campy once had a run-in with a Manchester catcher, who threw dirt in his face. Campy tore off his mask and warned him, "If you ever do anything like that again, I'll beat you to a pulp."

Campanella was productive at Nashua. He drove in 96 runs in 113 games and hit 13 home runs. In fact, there was a man in Nashua who was in the poultry business, and as a promotion he would give 100 baby chicks to a player for every home run he hit.

Campy earned 1,300 baby chicks. And to this day, I'm still trying to figure out what a man who lived in the middle of Harlem did with 1,300 baby chicks.

I became the general manager of the Montreal Royals in 1948, a promotion that came as somewhat of a surprise to me. In fact, had I not enjoyed a good drink from time to time, I might inadvertently have turned down the best front-office job in the Dodger organization, aside from Branch Rickey's position.

When Larry MacPhail was with the Dodgers, he always kept several bottles of liquor in his desk drawer. Mr. Rickey, on the other hand, detested drinking. At the time, the Dodgers had three Class AAA clubs—Hollywood, St. Paul, and Montreal. Mr. Rickey called me in one day and asked, "Buzzie, how would you like the Canadian club?"

"Well, yes sir, Mr. Rickey," I said. "If you don't want it, I'll take it." I thought he meant a bottle of leftover liquor, Canadian Club, from Larry Mac-Phail's old desk. I was serious. Mr. Rickey didn't think that was very funny.

I honestly considered declining the promotion anyway. Evit and I had just bought a house in Scarsdale because I'd been told I would be working in the Brooklyn office. But Mr. Rickey convinced me to accept the Canadian job with an offer I thought I could not afford to refuse.

"Young man, that job will be worth $25,000 to you some day," Mr. Rickey said, needing to say no more. I was making $5,000 at the time. I went home and told Evit that we had no choice. We had to take it. I would get an immediate raise to $7,500. Three years later, I finally figured out how the job could be worth $25,000. Oh, it was worth that, all right: the three years in Montreal I made $7,500, $8,500, and $9,000. Exactly $25,000.

We had three exceptional years in Montreal. All 21 of the players from our 1948 team went to the major leagues, including Duke Snider, Carl Erskine, and Don Newcombe. We won the Little World Series and I was named the minor league Executive of the Year. The club made about $600,000, of which Mr. Rickey received 10 percent, unbeknownst to me until later. For my efforts, I received a $1,000 raise.

Everything clicked for us in Montreal, on and off

the field. For instance, inside the ballpark was a roller rink where we charged 50 cents for skates and admission. When the city decided to put a 30 percent tax on the admission price, we charged 10 cents for admission and 40 cents for the skates. The city, then, got only 3 cents per person instead of the 15 cents it had expected.

One of our best fans was John Stormont, the largest liquor distributor in the Dominion of Canada. He was known to all his friends as Sir John, and was so introduced to Mr. Rickey as Sir John. Sir John loved baseball, and every Saturday he'd come into my office with two bottles of Dewars Ne Plus Ultra Scotch, one for me, which I put away, and one for himself to consume during the game.

In 1930, Sir John went to New York with $2 million ticketed to help Franklin Delano Roosevelt become president. He was told by acquaintances to donate the money to Jim Farley, later the Postmaster General. Instead, he gave the money to Joe Kennedy, who in 1938 became U.S. ambassador to Great Britain. To repay him for his generosity, Kennedy gave Sir John Canadian rights to all the Scotch coming from Scotland.

Mr. Rickey thought Sir John was a terrific fan and he enjoyed sitting with him at Montreal games. But, until the day he died, Mr. Rickey, a teetotaler, thought Sir John had been knighted by the king. He never knew he ws a liquor salesman who was simply called Sir John.

Chuck Connors, who later became an actor and starred in the television series "The Rifleman," played for me at Montreal. He was a good minor league player, but his heart was elsewhere. He longed for a stage and screen career. Every spring in Vero Beach, Florida, he would recite "Casey at the Bat" to the 600 people there.

"Two things Mr. Rickey likes," Chuck once said, "are money and baseball players. But he never lets them get together."

Chuck was a first baseman and a pretty good left-handed hitter. He used to hit baseballs onto the roof of the building across the street from the Montreal park.

One October, prior to the opening of the Little World Series in which we were playing against the Dodgers' St. Paul club, the Royals were invited by the Montreal Canadiens hockey team to a hockey game. I was sitting next to Connors, who had a bandage around his little finger. He said, "I don't think I can play tomorrow."

"What do you mean?" I asked.

"I don't think I can swing a bat. It really hurts."

In the second period of the hockey game, the Canadien goaltender, Bill Durnan, was hit in the head with the puck. Goaltenders did not wear masks in those days, and Durnan's face was a mess. He was bleeding severely, the game was stopped, and he was taken into the clubhouse for eight stitches over his eye. After a few minutes, Durnan returned to the ice, which the public address announcer duly noted by declaring that even with eight stitches over his eye, Durnan was going to play.

When I heard that, I looked over at Connors, who was quietly removing the bandage from his pinkie. He played the next day.

One year we trained in the Dominican Republic. At the hotel built expressly for the Montreal ball club, I had the Generalissimo Suite. I was charged $11 a day, three meals included for a suite that had a living room, a bedroom, a porch, a dining room, a kitchenette, and a bathroom in which I could see myself in the mirror 56 times.

One day, Connors decided to have fun with a rookie.

He pointed to a policeman and told the kid to say, "You dumb son of a bitch. I'll knock you on your damn ass."

"Si, si, señor," said the policeman, who did not understand a word of English.

But the next day, the kid decided to repeat the scene. He walked up to a policeman and said, "You dumb son of a bitch. I'll knock you on your ass."

"You will, huh?" the policeman said. "Come with me."

This was a different policeman, one who understood English perfectly. It cost me $50 to get the kid out of jail.

Connors had one at-bat with the Dodgers, in 1949. They were playing the Giants at the Polo Grounds. The game was tied, it was the top of the eighth inning, and the Dodgers had runners on first and second with one out. Pinch-hitting, Connors hit a one-hopper to the second baseman, who turned it into a double play. As Connors hit first base, he kept on running, toward the clubhouse located beyond the centerfield fence.

"Where you going, Chuck?" Jake Pitler, the first-base coach, yelled.

"To Montreal," Chuck yelled back. And he was right. He was sent back to Montreal and was later traded to the Cubs.

In 1948, Mr. Rickey decided to venture into the football business, fielding the Brooklyn Dodger football team. He enlisted my services as a scout, which, needless to say, was an abject failure. My expertise in football did not extend beyond the fact that I knew a touchdown was worth six points.

One time, he sent me to see Mansfield State play Slippery Rock. He was of the opinion that by scouting small schools, we might find a player overlooked by other clubs, which scouted primarily major colleges.

I went to the game on Saturday, and on Monday morning I met with Mr. Rickey, who asked what happened.

"It rained a little bit," I said. "The field was wet and Slippery Rock won, 7-6."

"What else?"

"What do you mean what else?"

"Who looked good?"

"I don't know. I just watched the game. It was 7-6."

Another time, he sent me to Mississippi, armed with a check for $3,000, to meet with the father of All-American quarterback Charlie Conerly. After waiting my turn, I introduced myself and said I was representing Branch Rickey.

"Oh, my son would like to play in New York some place," Mr. Conerly said. "What's your offer?"

"I've got money with me," I said, and I handed him the check for $3,000.

"Did you see that fellow who just walked out of here?" Mr. Conerly said "He works for the Detroit club. He offered us $50,000 and we turned him down."

Conerly eventually signed with the New York Giants for about $60,000. So much for my time in football.

Another offer almost sidetracked me from baseball for good. At the end of the Montreal season in 1950, I was returning to Scarsdale, and at Grand Central Station in New York I ran into Ford Frick, then the president of the National League.

"You're just the man I want to see," he said. He explained how the Maytag family, who made the washing machines, wanted him to go to Colorado Springs to run the newspaper it owned there.

"I told Mr. Maytag I'd go if I could get the right

people to go with me," Mr. Frick said. "I want you to be the business manager."

"I don't know anything about the newspaper business," I said.

"There's nothing to it. It's just like running a baseball club."

This was Friday. Evit and I were going to the Fricks for dinner on Sunday night. In between, we discussed the offer at length, and Evit said, "We love the Fricks very much. He's been like a father to you since your dad died. But working with him might spoil our beautiful friendship." I was afraid she might be right.

On Sunday night, I declined the offer. Mr. Frick picked up the phone, called Mr. Maytag, and said he was not interested.

And I'm glad he did. A few weeks later, at the baseball winter meetings, Mr. Frick was named commissioner of baseball. And I was named the executive vice president of the Dodgers.

3

Baseball in Black and White: The Robinson Era

Major league baseball finally opened the doors to its exclusive club in 1947, discovering that black and white do mix. Jackie Robinson, of course, was the man who broke the color barrier, first playing for the Brooklyn Dodgers in 1947. Until the day Robinson died, he gave exclusive credit to Branch Rickey for enabling him to become the first black to play in the major leagues. In the process, he perpetrated what I feel is a significant oversight, as well as an injustice. Jackie never had any nice words to say about Walter O'Malley, which simply was not fair. Walter had as much to do with Jackie's reaching the big leagues as did Branch Rickey. This is the only problem I have with Jackie. Robinson was the best competitor I've ever seen, but he never gave Walter O'Malley the credit he deserved. Then again, no one did. It was always, 'Mr. Rickey did this and Mr. Rickey did that.' And he did. Mr. Rickey was the one who found Jackie: he set out to find the best black player, one who could physically play major league baseball and mentally withstand the abuse he was certain to take. The man he found was Robinson.

For whatever reason, Jackie was under the impression that Mr. Rickey was the only one involved in his ascension to the big leagues. But Walter O'Malley and John Smith, who along with Jim Mulvey and Branch Rickey owned the Dodgers at the time, had an equal say in the matter. Although Walter owned a one-fourth interest in the club, he had John Smith's voting power on baseball matters, giving him a 50 percent interest. Had Walter voted against Jackie, he would not have played for the Dodgers.

Others in our organization thought a young pitcher with the Newark Eagles was the right man. But Mr. Rickey vetoed Don Newcombe because of his age, 19.

In fact, long before Jackie Robinson played for Brooklyn, Walter O'Malley had entertained the notion of bringing a black player to the major leagues. Mr. O'Malley had gone by himself to Havana, Cuba, in 1944 to scout a black shortstop, Silvio Garcia, who at one time had been one of Cuba's best players. By the time O'Malley saw him, however, Garcia was simply too old to play major league baseball. Three years earlier, in 1941, Leo Durocher, managing the Dodgers at the time, had seen Garcia play and proclaimed on the spot, "If I could just paint him white, I could use him right now."

Happy Chandler, the commissioner, once said that Mr. Rickey received too much credit. He was right. Four people had roles in deciding Robinson was the right player to undertake the task of integrating the major leagues, including myself. I was assigned to look into Robinson's background, to make certain he was a man of impeccable character. Branch Rickey, Jr.'s assignment was to work closely with the 11 New York newspapers to gauge their attitudes, to see how they would react. Clyde Sukeforth's job was to follow

Jackie everywhere he went while he was playing for
Montreal in 1946, to see whether Robinson was physically capable of playing in the major leagues. And
Branch Rickey's job was to see that we had the right
player.

My job was the easiest. Mr. Rickey asked me to
search Jackie's background to see "if there is anything whatsoever that might embarrass the ball
club," he told me. I think the reason Mr. Rickey
selected me for this particular assignment was the
fact I knew nothing about Jackie at all, because I had
been in the army. He was seeking a fresh viewpoint
from someone unfamiliar with Robinson, for to know
him and to talk with him was to like him.

As soon as I met Rachel Robinson, Jackie's wife, I
knew there could not be anything wrong with Jackie.
She was one of the most remarkable women I'd ever
met. She was straightforward, honest, and beautiful.
You knew immediately that she wasn't going to make
a mistake in choosing her partner. As far as I was
concerned, that was all the investigating I needed to
do.

Still, I spoke with Mack Robinson, Jackie's brother,
the man who placed second to Jesse Owens in the 100-
meter race in the 1936 Olympics in Berlin. I spoke
with several people in California, many of whom
said, "If he's a brother of Mack's, then he's all right."

Sukeforth was given an easy task, too. He watched
Jackie play virtually every day for more than a year.
When he first saw Jackie play, he knew immediately
that he had sufficient talent. Sukeforth, in fact, said
it was senseless to send Robinson to the minors in
Montreal for a year, that he was ready to play for the
Dodgers in 1946. Realistically though, Robinson
needed to gain some experience under the spotlight
in an environment where the pressure wouldn't be so
great. In Montreal, race was not an issue.

Branch Rickey, Jr., had perhaps the toughest task.

He had to find out whether the newspapermen would make it easy for Jackie. Some of them had every intention of making it tough on him—until their newspaper instincts took over. A black player made great copy, and created a lot of debate and controversy. It could be a newspaperman's gold mine.

Finally, there was the matter of the commissioner, Happy Chandler. The Dodgers had kept their plans and their new player a secret until the last possible moment. Happy Chandler had very little to do with the historic event. Yet, he has frequently taken credit for Jackie Robinson's entry into baseball.

In Peter Golenbock's book, *Bums*, Chandler said, "I had a role in Robinson's breaking the color line just like Rickey, though Rickey tried to take all the credit for that, and in that I was disappointed. . . ."

Ridiculous. The decision about Jackie Robinson was made by the Brooklyn Dodgers ownership and *only* the ownership. Chandler was informed of the Robinson matter as a courtesy to his office.

In 1946, the Montreal Royals and Jackie Robinson debuted in Jersey City. A crowd of 52,000, most of it there to see Robinson, witnessed a sign of things to come. Robinson had four hits, including a home run, and stole two bases. That year, the Royals won the International League pennant, and Robinson led the league in hitting at .349.

On April 10, 1947, a press release passed out in the Ebbets Field press box, stated, "Brooklyn announces the purchase of the contract of Jack Roosevelt Robinson from Montreal. He will report immediately."

And when the color barrier finally fell, so did a myth created by a New York sportswriter, who had written that "Blacks have been kept out of big league ball because they are as a race very poor ballplayers." As a 28-year-old rookie, Robinson batted .297 and led

the league in stolen bases with 29. He was the
National League's Rookie of the Year and finished
fifth in MVP balloting.

Two years later, in 1949, Robinson was the league's
MVP, edging the Cardinals' Stan Musial. He batted
.342, with 203 hits, 122 runs scored, 124 runs batted
in, and 37 stolen bases. He would bat over .300 six
straight years. He wasn't the best ballplayer I've
seen, though on any given day he was a great player.
But as a competitor, he was without equal, the best I
have ever seen. Pete Rose is a competitor, but he
doesn't have the kind of ability Jackie had. I'm
talking about a man who, with two outs in a close
game, would steal home. Jackie stole home 20 times
in his career.

Robinson was as good as any second baseman in the
league. He did not have the range of a Charlie
Gehringer or the power of a Tony Lazzeri. He did not
have particularly great speed. But put it together,
and add an unparalleled competitive nature, and you
had an exceptional player. Jimmy Cannon, a noted
sportswriter of that era, once said, "If Jackie were
white, he'd be another Enos Slaughter." He was
right. And both are in the Hall of Fame.

Jackie was both outspoken and private. He was the
type of person who would speak his mind publicly,
without regard to whether he was hurting people.
Then, once he realized he had hurt someone's feelings, he'd privately write them a letter of apology the
next day. He'd pop off about an owner or a manager
or another player. The newspapers would run banner
stories. The following day, Jackie would send his
letter of apology. Well, a million people saw the
newspaper story. Only one person saw the apology.

At the end of his career, Robinson once crossed the
wrong man. No letters would ever mend the hurt
Walter O'Malley experienced from Robinson's lack of

courtesy in informing the club of his retirement plans.

When Robinson elected to retire before the 1957 season, he failed to inform anyone but *Look* magazine, which had paid him a significant sum of money for the story. Meanwhile, we had decided to trade him. Knowing Jackie, we didn't think he'd go anywhere but New York, so we worked out a deal with the Giants. We gave them Robinson and received in return $50,000 and Dick Littlefield.

We were certain Robinson would be happy with this trade. He would be staying close to his home in Stamford, Connecticut. The announcement of the trade was made. A few days later, *Look* and its story of Robinson's retirement reached the newsstands.

Jackie insisted that his retirement was a last-minute decision that came as a result of the trade, but that wasn't likely. Magazines aren't published overnight. He and *Look* magazine had to have arranged their deal long before. As a result, I would say that Robinson knew he was going to retire before we announced that we had traded him.

The Giants complicated the issue by offering Robinson $60,000, far more than he ever made as a Dodger. For awhile, he was tempted to take the offer, though *Look* magazine undoubtedly would have screamed.

As a matter of fact, I've often thought that if Jackie had elected to play for the Giants, the club might not have moved from New York to San Francisco. That's how much Robinson would have helped them at the gate. And they needed help.

Jackie and I were never close, although despite what has been written, no significant friction ever existed between us. He simply was not an outgoing sort. He would never stop by the office to talk baseball like a Drysdale or a Hodges or a Campanella or an Erskine.

Nevertheless, I respected the man and I have even come to his defense. I remember one time when Harry Caray, then the radio broadcaster for the St. Louis Cardinals, made some derogatory remarks about Jackie, I wrote Harry a nasty letter.

A few days later, he phoned me and said, "I have a right to say what I want. I'm a reporter first and a broadcaster second."

"Then why don't you say what you really think about Busch beer?" I asked.

The Cardinals, of course, were owned by the Busch family.

"What do you mean?" Harry asked.

"I heard you ordering Schlitz. Why don't you say that on the air, that you prefer Schlitz to the product produced by your employer?"

"I can't do that."

"Why not? You're a reporter first, right?"

Finding something derogatory to say about Robinson's playing ability took some imagination. No one can say that Jackie ever dogged it. In fact, one of the Dodgers' concerns was that he played too hard.

It was too bad it all ended the way it did. Walter O'Malley took it all as a personal affront to the club. He felt it was an embarrassment to the Dodgers. You didn't do things like that to Walter O'Malley. I don't think he and Jackie ever spoke to each other again.

4

Rickey and O'Malley: A Pair of Kings

I was fortunate to have known both Branch Rickey and Walter O'Malley, although they would not always consider themselves fortunate to have known each other. They did not get along well.

In fact, by the time Walter had bought Mr. Rickey's stock in the Brooklyn Dodgers, the two were engaged in a bitter feud. After the Dodgers had moved to Los Angeles, Walter initiated a rule within the Dodgers offices: Anyone mentioning Branch Rickey's name would be subject to a $1 fine. The rule was meant as a joke, of course. At least, the rest of us considered it a joke, because anyone who did not mention Mr. Rickey from time to time probably was not too smart. He was a brilliant baseball man.

The issue behind their feud was money. At the time, neither had an abundance of it, at least not by ownership standards. As a result, Rickey was known as El Cheapo, a name given him by New York newspapermen. O'Malley was merely known as cheap.

But that wasn't really an accurate description of Walter. Every dime he made he put back into the Dodgers. As a matter of fact, cash flow once became such a problem that I offered to lend him money. At the time, he was cheap only because he didn't have the money to be anything else. And if you cheated Walter O'Malley out of 15 cents, you were in trouble, and rightfully so. He worked hard for his money.

Mr. Rickey's contract as president of the Dodgers expired after the 1950 season, and by then it had become evident that Walter wished to buy the one-fourth interest in the club his nemesis held. It would give him 50 percent of the Dodgers and a controlling interest.

The handwriting was on the wall, and Mr. Rickey could read. He knew that eventually he would be phased out entirely, that Walter would want the club to himself. So Branch elected to sell.

He had purchased his share for $320,000, as had Walter. When it came time to sell, Mr. Rickey's asking price was $1 million. O'Malley, meanwhile, offered only the price Mr. Rickey had originally paid for his stock.

The 1943 partnership agreement included a clause that became a most effective negotiating tool for Mr. Rickey. He found a buyer, real estate tycoon William Zeckendorf, who allegedly was offering Mr. Rickey $1 million for his stock. The clause gave Walter the right of first refusal.

Thus, Walter wound up paying $1 million for Mr. Rickey's stock. In adherence to the clause in the partnership agreement, Walter also had to pay the would-be buyer an additional five percent agent's fee of $50,000. Some suspect that Zeckendorf never really intended to buy Mr. Rickey's stock, that he was a pawn employed by Branch to get O'Malley to ante up $1 million. And as far as Walter was concerned, the additional $50,000 was a slap in the face.

Walter framed the canceled $50,000 check and placed it on a wall of his office, as a constant reminder. And it was that check that really fueled the feud. Though they had never been especially close, they had at least considered each other friends. Walter felt he was being cheated out of $50,000 by a friend.

That October, I was handling the Dodgers' allotment of World Series tickets and I was in the office working on it for Mr. Rickey. As Mr. Rickey was leaving, he put an envelope in my coat pocket and said, "Buzzie, read this tomorrow."

The letter said he was leaving the Dodgers to become the president of the Pittsburgh Pirates, and that he wanted me to go with him. It was tempting. Mr. Rickey was a great baseball man, and it would have been a great opportunity for me to keep working with him in the Pittsburgh organization. But because of my long relationship with the Dodgers, I felt I couldn't go. But he was a great man.

He almost never picked up a tab, though I'll never forget one time he did. Fresco Thompson, who began working for the Dodgers shortly after I did, went on a business trip with Mr. Rickey and me to Fort Worth, Texas. Fresco didn't want to go and was miffed the entire time.

We arrived at 6 A.M. and went to breakfast, and much to our surprise, Mr. Rickey was going to buy. But when we went to the cash register, he had somehow misplaced the check.

"You don't need the check," a still-irked Fresco told the cashier. "Just look at his tie and you can tell what he had to eat."

When I first took over as general manager of the Dodgers in 1951, Mr. Rickey, now with the Pirates, was the first to call me to discuss player personnel. He wanted to buy a player from the Dodgers.

"Who's that, Mr. Rickey?" I asked.

"Oh, that young fellow at Montreal. I don't know what his name is. It begins with an M, I think, an infielder." He knew very well what his name was.

"You mean Bobby Morgan?"

"That's the young man, that's who it is. I'd like to buy him." He offered me $50,000.

"Wait a moment, Mr. Rickey." I put down the phone and began to shuffle through some papers in the desk. When I found what I was looking for, I returned to the phone.

"I couldn't take a penny less than $150,000 for him."

"Judas priest, young man, where'd you get that figure?" he asked, obviously shocked.

"Mr. Rickey, I'm using your old desk, and in it I found a listing of the amount you expected to receive for each and every player. Your price on Morgan was $150,000."

Like anyone who knew Branch Rickey, I learned a great deal about the baseball business from him. He was the finest baseball man I ever met. Everyone who knew him will tell you the same thing. He could predict the future of a raw youngster as well as anyone ever could.

One time, he gave me a lesson in the art of wheeling and dealing, though this time it was more wheeling than dealing.

"I want to show you how to make a deal. John Galbreath [the owner of the Pittsburgh Pirates] is coming into town to see me. He wants Duke Snider. How much do you think Snider is worth?"

I said he was worth maybe $200,000.

"I'll show you how to get it up to $400,000," Mr. Rickey said. "You sit over there and don't say a word."

Mr. Galbreath arrived, and he and Mr. Rickey talked for a few minutes. Mr. Galbreath said, "Branch, I don't have much time. But you know why I'm here."

"Before we get into that," Mr. Rickey said, "you've got a pitcher there that I'd like to have, Bill Werle."

Werle hadn't had a very good year and was on his way out of baseball. I couldn't understand why Mr. Rickey wanted him.

"Now, John, I'll give you $200,000 for Werle," Mr. Rickey said, writing down the offer on an envelope. Then I knew what Mr. Rickey was doing. By judging a player of Werle's limited abilities to be worth $200,000, he implied that Snider was worth at least $400,000. Mr. Rickey had artificially increased Snider's worth by $200,000.

"I can't do anything about this now," John said, putting the envelope in his pocket. But the point was made. We could never have paid $200,000 for Werle anyway: we didn't have but $50,000 or so in the bank. Still, there was the matter of the envelope with the written offer. So the next morning Mr. Rickey summoned the Dodgers' road secretary, Harold Parrott, who soon would be en route to Chicago with the ball club.

"Harold, you get off the train in Pittsburgh," Branch told him. "Mr. Galbreath's got an envelope I'd like to have back."

Mr. Rickey was not about to pay $200,000 he did not have for a pitcher who could not pitch. When Harold arrived in Pittsburgh and went to see Mr. Galbreath, John said, "I know what you want," and he handed Harold the envelope.

Aside from his reputations as a superb baseball

mind and a cheapskate, Branch Rickey had another reputation well deserved. He was known as a teetotaler, and he detested the consumption of alcoholic beverages by others.

My favorite Branch Rickey story is a familiar one that has been told countless times, though infrequently with the right attribution. Mr. Rickey was the originator of this story, and I was a witness.

It involved a fine minor league pitcher named Henry Behrman. We had signed him for $75 a month and he had played for me at Valdosta. Eventually he was sold to Pittsburgh for $50,000.

Just before Mr. Rickey left the organization, he called Henry into his office. Henry was a young fellow who had a tendency to drink a little bit. With Mr. Rickey, even a little bit was too much.

"We've got to teach this young man a lesson," Branch said to me. "He's got a great arm, but he's got to take care of himself. We've got to show him how liquor is not only ruining his ability to play baseball, but also his health."

When Henry arrived, Mr. Rickey took out an old cigar box filled with dirt and a few worms. He took one worm out and put it in a glass of water.

"Come here, Henry. Look at that worm. What is it doing?"

"What do you mean 'what is it doing?' "

"What's it doing?"

"It's wiggling around."

Next, Branch put a worm in a glass of pure alcohol. Then he said, "Now tell me, Henry, what is the worm doing now?"

"It's not doing anything," Henry replied. "It looks like it's dead."

"You're right, son. Does that tell you anything?"

"No."

"Think about it a minute. Now tell me, Henry, what does it tell you?"

"Oh," he said, "now I know. If you drink a lot of booze, you won't get worms."

Walter O'Malley's forte was business, and he was the man responsible for the Dodgers' having the powerful public relations machine they have today. Walter's theory on public relations was to go to whatever lengths it took to get people in the seats. Good public relations translated to more business, and to Walter, baseball was a business. He made it a business for everybody, because as the Dodgers succeeded, the other clubs did too.

He never missed a trick. Anything that might boost business was worth looking into. For instance, Brooklyn was home to approximately 1.5 million Jewish people, and the Dodgers at the time did not have a Jewish person playing ball or even working for them in the front office. The O'Malleys were Catholic. I was Catholic. Red Patterson was Catholic. Fresco Thompson was Catholic. Although Brooklyn was a city of churches, they obviously weren't all Catholic churches. So Walter figured we'd better have someone of the Jewish faith in the organization.

Well, at that same time, Harold Parrott, our road secretary and another Catholic, got tired of traveling and asked for another assignment. Lee Scott, who had worked for a newspaper that had recently folded, was named our road secretary. We thought Scott was Jewish, because he was married to a lovely Jewish girl.

One morning in February, Scotty came in with a big black mark on his forehead.

"What's that, Scotty?" Walter asked him.

"Walter, you know today is Ash Wednesday. I just came from Mass."

His real name was Scotto. He was of Italian descent and was a good Catholic. We were right back where we started.

Walter never did find the quality Jewish player he sought until the club moved to Los Angeles, where it didn't matter. Koufax was Jewish, but he did not become a star until the club was in Los Angeles.

He thought he had the player in Cal Abrams, who not only was Jewish, but was from Brooklyn. We opened this particular season on the road, and Abrams had about 14 hits in his first 20 at-bats. Everyone was excited.

When the club finally got home, Dressen put Abrams in centerfield, and he went hitless in about his first 15 at-bats. He turned out to be an average outfielder who went from one club to another.

Walter almost never interfered in decisions on player personnel. All he asked was that we sell enough players each year to pay for the operation of Dodgertown in Vero Beach, Florida.

The first major decision I had to make involved an offer that would have put $650,000 in the Dodgers' depleted coffers. Walter called me in one day and said that Bob Carpenter, the owner of the Philadelphia Phillies, wanted to give us $650,000 and five players of little note if we would give him any two of three players—Gil Hodges, Duke Snider, or Roy Campanella. Remember, Walter had put all his money into the club, and a sum like that would have been a windfall.

"Walter, we can't do that," I said. "We will have $650,000 in the bank, but we won't win the pennant. If we don't make the deal, we'll win the pennant and make more than $650,000 and still have the players."

Fortunately, Walter turned Mr. Carpenter down. It was undoubtedly a tough decision for him to make. He had his life savings invested in the club, and that was a lot of money to walk away from. But he knew what was good for the club.

When it came to money, Walter was shrewd. He wasn't cheap. If he felt something was worth $200,

he'd give you $200 for it. If he felt it was worth only
$100, you'd get only $100. By the same token, if
something was worth $200 and he thought he could
get it for $100, he'd make every effort to acquire it for
the cheaper price. When it came to business, he was
without peer.

"If Walter O'Malley, instead of Kennedy, had been
negotiating with Khrushchev, Moscow would be a
Dodger farm club," said former Dodger publicity
man Irv Rudd.

Ralph Branca, the former Dodger pitcher, married
the daughter of Jim Mulvey, and the Mulvey family
owned 33⅓ percent of the club when it moved to Los
Angeles. Jim had passed away and the family was
getting nothing out of the club. Dividends weren't
paid, because Walter was putting all the money back
into the club. When Jim was alive, he was drawing a
salary of about $36,000 a year, and that was it. Not a
very good return on his investment.

So the family elected to sell its stock to Walter, and
Branca called me to seek my advice.

"We went in to see Walter," Ralph said to me, "and
he offered us $3 million for our one-third shares."

I thought about it quickly: 125 acres in Vero Beach,
300 acres here. The land alone was worth more than
that.

"'That sounds like a fair offer to me, Ralph, but why
don't you do this. Go in to Walter and say, "Walter,
instead of your giving us $3 million for our one-third,
we'll give you $6 million for your two-thirds."

"He won't do that," Branca said.

"Of course he won't. But ask him anyway."

He went in and did what I suggested. And he came
out with a pretty good offer from Walter, substan-
tially above the original $3 million.

Walter unquestionably was great for the game of
baseball. At times, he was suspected of running the
game from his Dodger Stadium office. He was ac-

cused of being the *de facto* commissioner of baseball, that Bowie Kuhn was a puppet and Walter controlled the strings. Walter never denied these allegations. I think he enjoyed them.

Walter had no more power than Mr. Wrigley or Mr. Galbreath or Mr. Autry or anyone else. But Walter was a lawyer and a businessman, and he was the first man to treat the game as a business. People would listen to him because they realized he knew what he was talking about.

Walter had a great story he enjoyed telling about himself. A young player, 18 years old, had died and gone to heaven, where St. Peter asked him, "What do you do?"

"I'm a ballplayer," the young man said.

"Oh, you'll like it up here, then. We have a lot of baseball players up here."

Two months later, the youngster had not yet found a baseball game, and he began to think to himself, "This isn't heaven." So he went back to see St. Peter.

"Where have you been looking?" St. Peter asked.

"All around."

"Did you go across the hill to a place called Chavez Ravine? You'll see games there."

The kid went there, looked down, and saw a hundred games going on. "Now this is heaven," he thought.

At bat one day, the youngster looked over to the dugout and there was a man standing there in a uniform and his foot on the top step of the dugout. He had the initials WOM on his cap. The kid looked at the umpire and said, "Gee, I didn't know Walter O'Malley was up here."

"That's not Walter O'Malley," the umpire said. "That's God. He thinks he's Walter O'Malley."

5

Walter Who? and Dressen, Too

Two of my favorite baseball men were the managers I hired for the Dodgers, both of whom helped set a precedent that would last 30 years. When Charley Dressen demanded a long-term contract after the 1953 season, the club instead hired Walter Alston as manager for the 1954 season.

Until he retired after the 1976 season, Alston always had one year contracts. It was a practice that continued with Tom Lasorda, until the club felt compelled to give him a three-year contract in 1984.

Dressen managed the Dodgers to National League pennants in 1952 and 1953, winning 105 games the latter year, and he asked for a three-year contract. You see, the Cardinals had given Eddie Stanky a three-year contract, the Giants had given Leo Durocher a two-year contract; Dressen felt he deserved a similar measure of security.

Dressen's wife, Ruth, wrote a letter to Walter O'Malley making unreasonable demands that included the three-year pact at $50,000 per year and an annual expense account of $10,000. This was not Walter's policy. No one received more than a one-year contract.

When Ruth's demands were not met, Charley came to me about the possibility of getting a two-year contract.

"Charley, I'm not going to do that," I said. "We've got a policy here and if we break it for you, we've got to break it for everybody. Listen, you've basically got a two-year contract anyway. In 1951, you tied for the pennant, so you're not going to get fired. Then, you won two straight pennants, so you're not going to get fired. You're entitled to have one bad year. So you've essentially got a two-year contract."

But Charley wouldn't buy it. He insisted on a multiple-year contract and instead wound up without even the one-year contract that had become a part of Dodger tradition.

They had been three delightful years with Dressen, and the success the Dodgers had with him at the helm was only part of it. Charley would talk baseball all day long—he really knew the game.

I loved having Charley around. He had innumerable jobs with several organizations during his career, but when he'd get fired he would always come back to me. I'd always have a job for Charley.

In 1963, he was working for me as a scout, and we'd sent him to watch the Detroit Tigers. One night, John Fetzer, the owner of the Tigers, and Jim Campbell, their general manager, called to inform me they were going to make a change, and were looking for someone to replace their manager, Bob Scheffing.

"We'd like to have Charley Dressen," Mr. Fetzer said.

"I don't know if Charley would take the job," I said. "We're both good friends of Bob's."

"Buzzie, isn't it better to have a friend of Bob's coming in here instead of someone who might criticize him?"

It made sense. The Tigers told me to make the deal myself, that whatever I worked out with Charley was fine with them. They knew, of course, I would not offer anyone more than a one-year contract.

I reached Charley in New York at 2 A.M. and I woke him up.

"Charley, what are you doing?" I said.

"Dammit, Buzzie, are you drunk?" he said. "It's 2 o'clock in the morning. I'm sleeping, what do you think I'm doing?"

"I don't mean that. What are you doing?"

"I'm doing what you told me to do. I'm following Detroit."

"How do they look?"

"There's not a damn player on this club that we want. They don't hustle, they don't do anything. They don't know how to play the game. We don't want any of them."

"In other words, you're telling me you might as well come home."

"Yeah, I might as well."

"Charley, I'll tell you what. I want you to manage that club."

"Are you sure you haven't been drinking, Buzzie?"

"No, I want you to manage that club. The Tigers asked me to talk to you about it, and they're going to pay you $35,000 a year."

"Are you serious? You want me to do that?"

I explained to him about Bob Scheffing and how the Tigers would prefer a friend of Bob's to take his place.

"Yeah, you'd better do it," I said.

"OK."

"Now, what about the Tigers, how do they look?"

"It's a damn good club, Buzzie. They've got Al Kaline. They've got Norm Cash . . ." The Tigers had suddenly become a great team.

Dressen was a stickler for discipline. He expected his players to observe a strict curfew, believing they could not carouse at night and play quality baseball the next day. And he went to extremes to see that they got their rest.

He knew all the tricks. If he knew someone would be staying out late, he'd plug the keyhole to his hotel room door, so he'd have to return to the front desk for help.

Sometimes Charley would leave a baseball with the night clerk at midnight and ask the clerk to have any players coming into the hotel to autograph the ball. When he would recover the ball the next morning, he'd know instantly the players who had been out too late.

Another time he made sure his players were all staying on the same floor with him. He took a chair from his room, put it out by the elevator, and just sat there, waiting for his players to come in late.

Charley fined Preacher Roe and Billy Cox for staying out late one night in St. Louis, but he announced to the press only that he had fined two players, unnamed. Seventeen wives called me in Brooklyn to find out if the guilty parties were their husbands. Two players were guilty, but seventeen were accused. That day, I made up my mind that any time we announced a fine, we would announce the player's name, too.

Regrettably, after three successful seasons as manager of the Dodgers, Charley had worn out his welcome with Walter O'Malley. "The Dodgers do not believe in long-term contracts," Walter said at a press conference.

A short time later, Charley got his three-year
contract, but it wasn't with the Dodgers. He signed a
three-year pact to manage the Oakland Oaks of the
Pacific Coast League.

The search for a new manager began in Louisville,
home of Dodger star shortstop Pee Wee Reese. Walter
O'Malley wanted someone the public could relate to,
as well as a man the players could respect. Reese
seemed to be the perfect choice.

He was Walter O'Malley's choice, too. "Fine, Walter," I said to him, "I'll talk to him. But let's make a
deal. If he doesn't want the job, we'll go for Walter
Alston." He agreed.

During the winter, I flew to Louisville and met Pee
Wee at the airport. We went to lunch and I asked him,
"Pee Wee, do you have an interest in managing?"

"Well, number one, I still think I can play some
more," he said. "Number two, we just won the pennant two straight years. How can you improve on
that? I don't think I'm ready to manage now."

That was the extent of our conversation. It has been
written that I talked Pee Wee out of taking the job for
the sake of bringing in my own man, Alston. That
was not the case. I *will* say that I did not try to talk
him out of his decision to refuse the offer. I felt Pee
Wee would eventually become a manager anyway. As
a matter of fact, when I was president of the San
Diego Padres, I offered him, through a third party,
the job of managing the club. But he was 60 years old
then and content with what he was doing.

Meanwhile, we had about 50 applicants for the
Dodger job, none of whom was Walter Alston. When
I asked him why he had not applied, he said, and I
quote, "Buzzie, you knew where I was." That was
Walter Alston. His approach was, "If you want me,
I'm here."

In the beginning, Walter O'Malley wasn't too sure he wanted Alston. He didn't know him, nor did he know much about him. In those days you simply did not hire managers with little or no major-league playing experience. Alston had had one at-bat in the major leagues, with the St. Louis Cardinals in 1936. He struck out.

O'Malley hired Alston entirely on my recommendation. Maybe I was going out on a limb, but I never thought so. I believed in what Alston could do. No matter which club we gave him, he had always done an excellent job. He did a great job at Trenton and Nashua. He won an American Association title at St. Paul in 1949. He won the International League championship at Montreal in 1951 and in 1952 and finished second in his other two years there, 1950 and 1953.

Still, few people had ever heard of him. But the fact he didn't have a reputation did not deter me. I hired him because he was a winner, which he had proven time and time again in the minor leagues.

On November 23, 1953, we decided to hire Alston. I called him at his home in Darrtown, Ohio, and told him to catch a plane to New York immediately. Before making an announcement to the press, we were going to hide Alston at the McAlpin Hotel in New York. Concerned that an aggressive newspaperman might discover Alston was registered there and prematurely break the story of his hiring, Walter O'Malley had a plan.

"Don't you think we ought to put him under an assumed name, so nobody knows he's there?" O'Malley suggested.

"Yeah, I will," I said.

"What name are you going to put him under?"

"Alston. That's an assumed name here. Nobody knows who Alston is."

Actually, we used the name Matt Burns, which

sounded suspiciously like a wrestling injury.
Strangely enough, the Dodgers had an employee
named Matt Burns.

When we finally announced that Alston would be
the new manager, the newspapermen were dumbfounded. The headline in the *Daily News* the next day
proclaimed:

ALSTON (WHO HE?)
TO MANAGE DODGERS

The writers hadn't heard much about Alston
either, and they could not understand how the de-
fending National League champions could put their
faith and their future in an unknown quantity who, in
his first trip to the major leagues 18 years earlier,
had struck out. Of course, they expected he would
strike out again.

Anybody who criticized or ridiculed Walter Alston's way of managing simply did not understand
the game of baseball. Alston always got the most out
of what he had. When he had the players, he won.
When he didn't have them, he lost. That's what
managing is all about. Earl Weaver proved that in
1986 when his Orioles finished last.

Two seasons into his regime, he silenced his critics.
In 1955, the Dodgers not only won the National
League pennant, they also won their first world
championship, beating the Yankees four games to
three in the World Series. The Dodgers would win
four world championships and seven National
League titles during Alston's 23 years as manager of
the Dodgers.

Alston signed 23 one-year contracts with the
Dodgers, and he usually had no idea what his salary
was until he received his first paycheck. He would
sign a blank contract, and at a later date I'd fill in the

numbers. He never argued. And I always made sure that Walter made more money than I did. If I was making $30,000, I'd give him $35,000. If I was making $35,000, I'd give him $40,000.

It has been written that the reason I hired Walter in the first place was that I could manipulate him and run the team the way I thought it should be run. It was said that I was the *de facto* manager of the Dodgers.

I was always amused by such accusations. It made me feel important. If I indeed was managing the Dodgers through Walter, then I was a pretty good manager, wasn't I?

Nothing was further from the truth. At no time did I ever suggest anything to Walter regarding his managing of the club. The only time I ever made a request was when we were shopping a player on the trade market and we needed to showcase him. Walter would do that for me.

All Walter ever asked of me was that I give him one coach of his choice, one man to whom he could be close. He had Joe Becker for a long time. Then he had Lefty Phillips. Then Preston Gomez.

Alston was a man's man. He would not back down from anyone. He and Jackie Robinson once nearly came to blows, in 1955, when Alston could no longer stand Robinson's criticisms of him.

On one occasion he challenged the entire team, including Frank Howard, who was 6'7" and 250 pounds. The Dodgers hadn't been playing too well and they had just lost another game in Pittsburgh. En route to the airport, several players began grumbling about the lack of air conditioning on the bus. Alston ordered the bus driver to pull over, then chastised the players for their attitude. He concluded by challenging any of them to step outside to "discuss" it with him, and he got off the bus and waited.

No one wanted any part of it, of course. Alston was tough.

In Vero Beach once, Sandy Koufax and Larry Sherry went out to get a pizza at 1 A.M., or so they said later. When they returned, they made some noise, and Walter heard them. He opened his door and saw Sherry sprinting toward the room. Walter went after him and banged on the door so hard that he broke his 1959 World Series ring. I'm surprised he didn't break the door down. Walter would never, never let you lie to him. If you lied to him, and he found out, you were in trouble.

Despite the series of one-year contracts, Alston had job security. Once Walter O'Malley knew Alston, he was an Alston man. But because of the one-year contracts, someone would speculate nearly every year that that year would be Alston's last.

During one spring training after a particularly poor season, Walter O'Malley invited Alston to go on a turkey shoot with him. The story spread throughout the camp: "One of the Walters is not coming back." I think O'Malley spread the story himself.

It was once said that Alston was 20 years of bad managing. That was a foolish thing to say. Alston was a great handler of pitchers, which he frequently proved, taking other teams' pitchers and getting quality work from them. Jim Brewer, Ron Perranoski, Bob Miller, Claude Osteen, and Phil Regan come to mind. Regan was 1–5 with the Cubs in 1965 and was 14–1 with the Dodgers in 1966.

On only two occasions in the 14 years Alston managed the Dodgers while I was with the club did we ever discuss making a change. The first time occurred during the 1958 season. Some of the players had trouble making the transition from Brooklyn to Los Angeles. They didn't seem to be generating the enthusiasm they had in Brooklyn.

I had begun to wonder whether it was Alston's
fault. Maybe he felt the same way. I didn't know. I
had a meeting with some of the players and coaches
to collect their thoughts on the matter. It was a
delicate situation, and I met with them on the sly,
without Alston's knowledge.

I met with Pee Wee Reese and Charley Dressen,
who had taken coaching positions with the Dodgers. I
let both of them know my feelings: I thought that the
club hadn't handled the move from New York well
and that they weren't taking it in stride. I also said
that I thought the club was out of hand.

Based on what I said, Pee Wee and Charley apparently thought the Dodgers wanted to fire Alston,
which wasn't necessarily the case. It was only an
option, and we were keeping our options open.

Both Pee Wee and Charley got mad, saying that
was the most ridiculous thing they'd ever heard.
Charley said, "If he goes, I go." That was enough for
me, because everybody assumed that when Charley
returned to the Dodgers as a coach, he did so with the
idea of replacing the man who replaced him as
manager.

The only time Alston was precariously close to
losing his job was in 1962, after the Dodgers lost a
four-game lead to the San Francisco Giants in the
final two weeks of the season and finished in a tie
after 162 games. The Giants won the playoff, two
games to one.

This was the only time Walter O'Malley ever discussed a managerial change involving Alston. We
were so disappointed, after coming so close, to lose
that pennant. It wasn't much different from the 1951
season.

Walter O'Malley had even brought up Leo Durocher, then a Dodger coach, as a possible successor.
I told Walter that if he was going to fire Alston, he'd

have to fire me, too. There was no way I was going to stay around without Alston.

Leo, in fact, was overheard second-guessing Alston and it nearly cost him his coaching job. Hank Greenberg was at a table near Durocher's in a restaurant shortly after the World Series, and he could hear Leo popping off about how he would have handled things differently. Hank called me the next day to tell me that it was embarrassing the way Leo had been carrying on.

A day later, at a dinner for the Dodgers at the Friar's Club, I saw Leo coming up the steps with announcer Vin Scully. Vin knew I was mad and wanted no part of it. He continued up the stairs.

I told Leo, "Don't you ever come near the ball club again. You're through. I don't ever want to have anything to do with you, you ungrateful SOB." Leo, meanwhile, claimed he had never said a word.

The next morning I phoned Walter Alston and said, "You need a new coach. I fired Leo."

"Don't do that," Walter said. "I like Leo. I like having him around." So I had to rehire him. Years later, I would hire him again, as a spring training consultant for the Angels. And if I were operating a club today, Leo would still be with me. He was good for the game.

Today, Leo lives in Palm Springs. He goes to church every Sunday and takes up the collection, which is fine. Leo swears the church gets it all.

When Alston finally retired, after the 1976 season, he was ready to retire. To those who questioned his ability, he could answer by pointing to 23 consecutive years on the job, four world championships, seven National League titles, and 2,040 wins, which ranks fifth on the all-time list.

Baseball would miss him. So many managers owe

Walter Alston a debt of gratitude, because until he became the Dodger manager, clubs simply would not hire minor-league managers with little or no major-league playing experience. Walter was the first.

Even when he was dying, he was still a baseball man. He was in love with the game. I used to call him twice a week and we'd talk baseball. How I miss those calls today.

6

The Brooklyn Years:
The Highs and
(Billy) Loes

These were the years I would not trade for any others, from my first year as the executive vice president of the Dodgers in 1951 until the club moved to Los Angeles after the 1957 season.

It was a remarkable era in Dodger history, and undoubtedly the most fun I've ever had in the major leagues. It was the last of the great eras, as far as I'm concerned. Roy Campanella said it recently: "Baseball changed with the evolution of the airplane" as the means of transportation. When baseball reached the west coast, trains were out and planes were in.

To this day, I still enjoy taking trains whenever I can. To me, the trains were an enjoyable and important part of baseball. When trains were the predominant form of transportation, we'd go from New York to Chicago on the Twentieth Century Limited and have our own dining room, club car, and two Pullman cars. The longest trip we made, from New York to St.

Louis, took 23 hours. Players would play cards for hours.

I was walking through the parlor car one day and several players were playing a game called Guess Who? The leader would provide a category and the initials of the person he had in mind and the others would attempt to guess the person. If someone guessed right, the leader had to pay $1 to each of them. If no one guessed the answer, they each had to pay $1 to the leader.

In this particular game, outfielder Gino Cimoli was the leader. The category was orchestra leaders and the man's initials were E.C. One of the players said, "Eddie Condon." No, it wasn't Eddie Condon. Another said, "Emil Coleman." No, it wasn't Emil Coleman.

After 10 minutes, they gave up, and Cimoli revealed the answer.

"Xavier Cugat," he said. Cimoli assumed Xavier began with E, because of the pronunciation. But that wasn't the funniest part. The other players paid Gino. They all thought Xavier was spelled with an E, too.

To me, that was baseball. Not 25 men sitting apart on a chartered airplane, reading the *Wall Street Journal* and knowing little about the men with whom they play every day.

New York baseball was never so intriguing and intoxicating as it was in the 1950s, when it gave us Willie, Mickey, and the Duke, roaming center fields at the Polo Grounds, Yankee Stadium, and Ebbets Field.

No greater rivalry ever existed than that involving the Brooklyn Dodgers and the New York Giants, unless it was the World Series with the Dodgers and the Yankees or the Giants and the Yankees.

These were years when for the first time the

Dodgers experienced the thrill of victory in the World Series and the ignominy of defeat.

My career in the major leagues began as I watched my first team take a 13½-game lead over the Giants on August 12, and lose it on the final day of the season. The Giants won 39 of their final 47 games, including 16 in a row at one point, to finish in a tie with the Dodgers, forcing a playoff. In the best-of-three playoff series, the Dodgers lost the third and deciding game, 5–4, on Bobby Thomson's "shot heard 'round the world," a three-run home run in the ninth inning. It was the the greatest comeback in baseball history, but the Dodgers were on the wrong side.

I'll never forget the day. It was October 3, 1951, my mother's birthday. I took the loss better than most, if only because I had not yet learned how difficult it was to win a pennant. My attitude was that we'll win one next year, which we did.

Everyone assumes this was the most disappointing moment in my career, but it wasn't. When the Angels led the 1982 American League Championship Series two games to none, only to lose three straight to Milwaukee, it hurt far more, if only because I wanted it so badly for Gene Autry.

We may have lost a 13½-game lead in 1951, but we played reasonably well. The Giants simply did not lose. Our players did their jobs until the final two weeks, when they let down somewhat. And every time we'd lose, the Giants would win. It was disappointing, to be sure, but you could see it coming. And I refuse to call it a collapse on our part.

Charley Dressen made the right decision in bringing Ralph Branca in to pitch to Thomson. It just turned out wrong. The situation was similar to the 1985 National League Championship Series when the Dodgers elected to pitch to Jack Clark of St. Louis in the ninth with first base open and Andy Van Slyke on deck. Clark hit a three-run homer and the series was over.

In 1951, first base was open, too, and Dressen chose to have Branca pitch to Thomson. The on-deck hitter was Willie Mays.

In retrospect, I'm not so sure I wasn't glad we lost. Had we won, I was expected to come up with 1,000 World Series tickets I didn't have for the mysterious "Man in the Gray Hat."

I first encountered the Man in the Gray Hat in Montreal. I was introduced to him by a man named Eddie Quinn, who promoted wrestling shows in Montreal. Eddie held one at our ballpark, which, incidentally, scared the devil out of me.

At the end of one exhibition—they couldn't call them matches in Canada—Yukon Eric hit his opponent over the head with a chair, and they carried the guy out. I got nervous, then. I was the landlord and I was afraid I'd be sued for everything we had.

"Damn, Eddie," I said, "you didn't have enough police out there. Why'd you let a thing like that happen?"

"Ah, don't worry," he said. "The guy will be wrestling tomorrow night in Ontario." It was all staged, of course, which I didn't realize at the time.

Eddie, meanwhile, had invited me to a barbecue at his house the next night, where I met this man wearing a gray felt fedora named Frankie Carbo, but called "The Man in the Gray Hat," or "Mr. Gray." He was involved in the boxing business.

Two years later, after I'd been promoted to Brooklyn, it appeared we were going to win the National League pennant. I got a call from Frankie Carbo.

"Frankie who?" I asked.

"Frankie Carbo." I had met him just once, two years earlier.

"Yes sir, Mr. Carbo, what can I do for you?"

"Well, it looks like you're going to win and I need some World Series tickets."

I assumed he wanted two tickets for himself, and I could handle that.

"I need a thousand tickets," he said. "I decided to make the boys in the fight racket give me a thousand apiece for them."

A thousand tickets at a thousand apiece is a million dollars. I began stuttering. I knew of his reputation and I didn't know what to say.

"Why don't you call me later," I said, buying time.

I then called Eddie Quinn and said, "Eddie, two years ago, you were kind enough to invite me to dinner at your house, where I met a fellow by the name of Frankie Carbo."

"Yeah, the Man in the Gray Hat."

"That's right. You know what he did? He just called me up and asked for a thousand tickets for the World Series. He wants to sell them for a thousand dollars each. I can't give him more than two tickets. What'll I do?"

"You're in trouble," Eddie said.

I often wake up in the middle of the night wondering what would have happened had we won the pennant and I had had to provide Frankie Carbo with 1,000 tickets I didn't have.

This was how I learned the value of tickets. At World Series time, one-hundred dollar bills are nothing. They come out of the woodwork. But we didn't have to worry about World Series tickets in 1951. They weren't ours to sell, because of Bobby Thomson.

Four years later, the Miracle at Coogan's Bluff was but a fading memory, and, in the aftermath of the Dodgers' first world championship, it was forgiven and forgotten. The 1955 Brooklyn Dodgers was the best team I ever had. Seven members of that club are on my personal All-Star team of players I employed: Gil Hodges (first base), Jackie Robinson (second base), Billy Cox (third base), Pee Wee Reese (shortstop), Duke Snider (outfield), Carl Furillo (outfield), and Roy Campanella (catcher). The only non-Dodger on my team is Dave Winfield (outfield). Doug DeCinces, based on his great 1982 season, is a close second to Cox at third base.

From the moment the Dodgers reported to spring training, you could sense that 1955 was to be something special. The club had enormous ability and two big reasons to excel: one, they were expected to win the pennant in 1954 but they didn't, and two, they had never won a World Series.

We had a great spring training, which carried over into the season. We won the pennant by 13½ games, and, although we lost the first two games of the World Series, we defeated the Yankees in seven games for Brooklyn's first and only world championship. Johnny Podres pitched an eight-hit shutout in the seventh game for the 2–0 Dodger victory.

The celebration was unforgettable. The town went wild, people unleashing years of pent-up frustration. At last, they no longer had to "wait 'til next year." Walter O'Malley threw a party at the Hotel Bossert in Brooklyn and expected maybe 600 people; about 1,200 people showed up.

Jack Lasculie, the announcer of the original "Tonight Show," wanted Podres to go to Manhattan to do the show, but I wouldn't allow it.

"He can't do that," I said. "He's not feeling well. He's had a few drinks, and I don't know what's he's liable to say."

They had hoped to entice him with a pretty blond who was working for the show. She was to escort Podres to Manhattan, riding with him in the back seat of the limo.

"That would make it worse," I said. "There's no way I'm going to let John go over there."

Thirty-one years after the party, Don Newcombe, a 20-game winner for the '55 Dodgers, reminded me that those boys were not all malted-milk drinkers. Most of them, like Podres, Roebuck, and myself included, enjoyed a drink or two, but never let it interfere with our desire to win a championship. In 1986, Newcombe was a guest on the pregame show of a nationally televised game, and he said he had been an alcoholic, an admission he has made frequently.

I've known Newcombe since 1946, over 40 years. He was with me when he played at Nashua and in Montreal and with the Dodgers. To this day, I have never seen him take a drink of alcohol. Never.

"Buzzie," Campanella told me, "I roomed with him all those years. I never saw him take a drink."

Today, Newcombe is the Dodgers' director of community relations. His alcohol problems presumably began after he had left the Dodgers at the end of the 1958 season. He is outspoken on the subject of alcohol and drug abuse, helping to keep both out of baseball and society.

The Dodgers of the fifties were many things, but they were never boring. One time, we were in Philadelphia battling for a pennant, and Newcombe had volunteered to pitch both games of a doubleheader. He won the first game, 2-1, and lost the second one, 2-1. The club left for Chicago after the game, arriving about 8 P.M.

Chicago, it should be noted, was the only city where Alston imposed a curfew, though he would not enforce it. He felt it was the responsibility of the players to adhere to it. Since Wrigley Field did not have lights and all the games were in the daytime and

Chicago bars were open until 4 A.M., Walter did not want his players out all night.

At about 10 o'clock that night, I thought I'd call Newcombe to tell him how much I appreciated what he had done by pitching both ends of the double-header. But he wasn't in his room. I called at 11 o'clock and he wasn't there. I called at midnight, 1 A.M. and 2 A.M., and he wasn't there. By then, I was annoyed.

Adding to my ire was the fact that I had spotted pitcher Ed Roebuck behind a bar, mixing cocktails for the customers. The next day, I went to the clubhouse and asked Walter if I could speak to the players. I told him what happened, and he agreed to let me talk.

"Here we are battling for the pennant and some of you fellows are staying out all night just because the manager doesn't believe in real curfews," I said. "Rather than embarrassing any of you, I want anybody who broke curfew last night to meet me in the men's room in 10 minutes."

I went outside and came back 10 minutes later, and I couldn't get into the men's room. Twenty-four of our 25 players were in there. What could I do? I started laughing. So much for discipline!

Still, I couldn't let Newcombe get away with it. I had a meeting with him, and explained how I had called him hourly last night to thank him for what he did for the club, but that he wasn't in his room.

"I was in the hotel," he said.

"But you weren't in your room."

Newcombe explained that he had indeed been in his room, however briefly. He had returned there to get his portable record player to take back to another room, where he was having a party.

"Buzzie, when I'm partying, I like to have some music," he said.

"Nevertheless, you weren't in your room, so I've got

to fine you. I'll give you your choice, $300 or three days' pay."

He was smart enough to know that $300 was less than three days' pay, so he was fined $300. Later on, when we were returning to Brooklyn by plane, I was sitting in front of Newcombe and Jim Gilliam. I was trying to sleep, but I could overhear them talking.

"You've got to be crazy," Gilliam said to Newk.

"What do you mean?" Newcombe said.

"For getting fined $300. What did you do it for?"

"It was worth it. We even had music."

"For $300," Gilliam said, "you could have hired your own orchestra."

Johnny Podres and Don Zimmer were two of the characters who made those days in Brooklyn so enjoyable. To this day I remain close to both of them. We all had a mutual interest, or mutuel interest as it were, in the race track. As a matter of fact, when Zimmer went to visit Podres in the hospital after John's heart attack last year, he stopped at the Saratoga track on the way and made a $20 bet for Podres. The horse won, and Zimmer showed up with $600 for John.

I wasn't quite that lucky with them. One time, when Podres and Zimmer were together in Detroit, they were going to Hazel Park, and they called me with a tip on a horse. The horse was a cinch, they said. It would go off at 7 to 1 odds.

"OK, bet $100 for me," I said.

"Oh, no, we owe you $200," one of them said. "Let us bet the $200."

I agreed, and when I hung up, I told my secretary, Edna Ward, that I had just lost $200.

"How do you know you'll lose?" Edna asked.

"I guarantee you I'll lose," I said. "They owe me $200 and are going to bet it on a horse, but they never told me the name of the horse."

The next morning, Podres and Zimmer called and

said, "Damn, the horse went off at 12 to 1, but we just got nipped at the wire."

That was 20 years ago, and I still haven't learned the name of the horse.

In Vero Beach, a 75-year-old man came with his dog every morning to watch practice and he'd sit on a rock by field No. 1, right outside the clubhouse. One morning he keeled over. We got the club doctor to look at him, but it was too late—the old man had died of heart failure.

Suddenly, Lee Scott, the road secretary, was going through the dead man's pockets. I thought maybe he was looking for identification.

"What the hell are you doing?" I said. "You can't do that."

"I've got to get the $40 back," he said.

"What $40?"

"Podres and Zimmer gave the guy $40 to bet for them, and they want it back."

The old man was the local bookmaker.

I fired Scotty once, temporarily. On June 15, 1955, the trading deadline, I called Scotty at the Stevens Hotel in Chicago to make sure he was available in case we made a trade.

"Oh, Mr. Scott said he did not want to be disturbed before 10 o'clock," the hotel operator told me.

"This is his office calling and it's very important," I said.

"I'm sorry, but he's a valued customer. We can't do it."

"Can I leave a message then? When he wakes up at 10 o'clock, tell him he's been fired."

I hung up. Five minutes later, the phone rang. It was Scotty.

One of the all-time characters of any era was Billy Loes, who probably is best known for losing a ground ball in the sun. At least, that is how he explained the

ground ball that went between his legs in the World
Series.

On another occasion, he fielded a ground ball and
threw it over the head of first baseman Gil Hodges.
"There was too much spit on the ball," he explained.

Loes was a pitcher of better than average skills. He
was one of the few men ever to coerce Branch Rickey
into opening his wallet. Mr. Rickey gave him a
$21,000 bonus, which was considerable in those days.

Loes never won more than 14 games in a season,
which he did only once. He never wanted to win 20
games, and he let everyone know it. He figured that if
he won 20 once, he'd have to do it again, and he'd be
expected to win 20 games every year. When we
traded him to Baltimore, he told the Orioles the same
thing.

In 1952, he won 13 games and lost eight, and I was
going to give him a raise to $17,000. But I said, "Billy,
you're not going to get the entire $17,000. I'm going to
take $400 a month out of your salary for six months
and I'm going to buy insurance for your mother and
daddy.

"Your daddy's a cripple. He's confined to a wheel-
chair. And your mother can't work, because she has
to take care of your daddy. You're an only child. So I
want to make sure they're protected if something
happens to you."

"Buzzie," Billy said, "I don't need any insurance. If
something happens to me, my mother and father
would commit suicide." He was serious.

Then he asked what I expected from him for
$17,000.

"Oh, I don't know," I said. "Maybe 14 wins."

When he won his 14th game in St. Louis in August,
he called me. "That's it. I'm going home," he said. He
figured he'd given the club its money's worth. He was
prepared to call it a year.

The subject of a pension came up one time, and

Billy had some thoughts on it. At that time, they were to receive $150 a month at age 55.

"Buzzie, what we should do is reduce it to about $125 a month and reduce the age so we can receive it at 45 instead of 55," Billy said.

"Billy, that makes sense," I said. "And people don't think you know anything except baseball. But why do you want to do that?"

"Because," he said, "who can make love when they're 55?" He wanted the money when he knew he could enjoy it.

Billy quit one day because I wouldn't buy him a dog. He quit another time because I wouldn't buy him a sports jacket. He would take $2 a day out of his $10-a-day meal money and buy a hamburger and a Coke. That's all he'd spend. He'd eat his other meals at the ballpark and save the rest of the money.

He was a funny kid. He came out to San Diego for an Old-Timers' game in 1976. We put up all the players at the Stardust Hotel, which has a golf course. Later, I received a bill from the pro shop for $360. I called over there and asked who was responsible for the bill.

"Billy Loes."

"Billy Loes? He doesn't play golf."

"No, it wasn't golf. He bought $360 worth of shirts."

"What did he do with them?"

"He sold them to the other players, at a discount."

We signed Roberto Clemente in the fall of 1953 and gave him a $10,000 bonus. In those days, if you paid a bonus of more than $4,000 to a player, you had to keep him on the big league club for a year, or risk losing him to another franchise in a draft.

At the time, the Dodger roster was so well stocked, the club simply did not have room for Clemente, despite his immense ability. So we attempted to hide him at Montreal. We did everything in our power to

ensure that Clemente would not shine. We did not
play him against left-handed pitchers, we played him
only against the best right-handed pitchers; he was
removed for a pinch hitter with the bases loaded in
the first inning of one game; he was benched the day
after hitting three triples in a game. It worked to an
extent—we kept his average down to .257.

Howie Haak, a Pittsburgh scout, went to Montreal
to see Clemente, and I offered to help him do his job.

"Stay in your room, Howie," I said. "You don't have
to watch the game. I'll give you the report on him."

Our efforts were for naught. Branch Rickey was
running the Pirates then, and Clyde Sukeforth had
left the Dodgers to scout for the Pirates. They were
aware of what was happening. On November 22,
1954, the Pirates drafted Clemente. We lost one of the
game's greatest players, a man who had 3,000 hits in
a very distinguished career.

Pee Wee Reese was involved in two of my favorite
spring training stories. One involved Rocky Nelson, a
pretty good hitter. Reese was on third, Rocky was the
hitter, and Reese was given the steal sign by Alston.
Rocky missed the sign and swung at the pitch, nearly
decapitating poor Pee Wee. Reese was steaming, and
he demanded an explanation.

"Why'd you swing?" Reese asked.

"Why do you think they call me Rocky?" Nelson
replied.

Another time, Reese, a quiet sort on the field, slid
into second base, and the umpire, George Mager-
kurth, who was about 6'5" and 280 pounds, called
him out. Reese thought he was safe. Pee Wee jumped
up and raised hell. The umpire walked away and
started to laugh.

After the game, I went down to ask the ump what
happened.

"I told him, 'Get back to the dugout or I'll bite your

head off,' " the umpire said. "Pee Wee said to me, 'If you do, you'll have more brains in your stomach than you've got in your head.' "

In those days, we would train in Vero Beach, and then move to Miami to play our exhibition games. The white players all stayed at the segregated McAllister Hotel. The black players stayed at the Lord Calvert.

After two years of this, I decided that if the McAllister Hotel would not accept our black players, we would move to another hotel. The manager of the McAllister acquiesced.

Campanella, Newcombe and Gilliam—the black players—got mad at me.

"What's the matter?" I asked.

"Come on over to our hotel and see," they said.

They each had suites by a swimming pool. The Lord Calvert was a beautiful hotel.

We had a similar problem in St. Louis. We finally convinced the Chase Hotel to allow our black players to stay there. Robinson was furious. The blacks had been staying at the Adams House, and people picked them up in Cadillacs, took them to the hotel, and treated them like kings.

In 1951, we were playing the Giants in the Polo Grounds when Willie Mays had just come up from the minor leagues. In the Polo Grounds, the club-houses were located beyond center field, so the opposing players often would walk to the dugouts together.

On this particular day, Campy and Mays were walking together and Campy had his arm around Willie, who was 20 at the time. He was telling Willie not to worry about anything.

"Today, Preacher Roe is pitching," Campy said. "He wouldn't hurt anybody. Now, tomorrow, Big

Newk [Newcombe] is pitching, and he don't like young blacks."

Campy is a beauty. He came in to see me one day in 1956, a year in which he made $33,000. He was smiling ear to ear, because he had just bought a house in Glen Cove on Long Island.

"That's fine, Campy," I said. "You can afford a house out there."

He told me he also bought a boat. I thought that was fine, too. He was living on Long Island Sound, and he could always use a little boat.

"Yeah, and I named it *Little Princess*," he said. He had named the boat after his daughter. Who puts a name on a row boat, I thought to myself suspiciously.

"What kind of boat is this?" I asked him. "How much did you pay for it?"

He had paid $56,000 for the boat, $4,000 more than he had paid for his house. In all, he had spent $108,000 and he didn't have 15 cents in the bank.

But players back then didn't care. At Nashua, Newcombe and Campy would get $87.50 each pay-day, twice a month. They'd get paid on the 15th and the next morning on the 16th, I'd see them at breakfast and they'd want to borrow $20.

"You just got paid," I said.

"Well, we put it in the bank."

"Take it out."

"We can't do that. It's bad luck to take it out of the bank."

Campy was as good a friend as I've had in this game, which proved fortunate for me one night. The Giants had just beaten Podres, 1-0, at the Polo Grounds, and I was so mad I started to walk to the hotel. Before I knew it, I was walking through the middle of Harlem at 11 o'clock at night. I started to worry, and began looking for a cab.

Campanella had a liquor store near where he had previously lived at 133rd and Lenox, and I was at 140th Street. Suddenly, I saw this couple coming toward me.

"Wait a minute, mister, wait a minute," the man said, and I thought I'd had it. I was thinking where I might kick him in self defense.

"You tell this black lady she should marry this black man," the man said to me. So I did. Who was I to argue? Then I continued walking. I got to 138th Street and saw this big, tough man coming toward me, and I said to myself, "Say your Hail Mary."

Before he reached me, I said, "Hey, mister."

"What do you want?"

"Do you know where Campanella's liquor store is?"

"What do you want it for?"

"Campy's a friend of mine."

"He's a friend of yours? I'll take you right there." And he escorted me to the store.

The fifties in New York provided all of us with fond memories and a favorite Yogi story. This is mine.

I was in Toots Shor's Restaurant after a Broadway show one night with Yogi, Allie Reynolds, and Red Smith of *The New York Times*. In walked Ty Cobb and his wife. Because of terrible arthritis, Cobb was using a cane. Somebody wondered aloud what Cobb would hit if he was still playing.

"Oh, about .375," Red Smith said.

"But the pitching isn't as good today," Reynolds said. "You've got one or two great pitchers and the rest are mediocre. I think he'd hit about .385."

"About .380," I said.

Now it was Yogi's turn.

"Oh, about .245," he said.

"Two-forty-five?" we said. "His lifetime average is .367."

"Yeah, but he's 72 years old," Yogi replied.

7

Coast to Coast:
The Move

My office was next to Walter O'Malley's office in
Brooklyn, at 215 Montague Street. He called me in
one day after the 1956 season and said, "Look down
there. What do you see?"

Across from our office was the welfare office. I
looked out the window and the problem was
apparent.

"I see a long, long line of poor Puerto Rican people
getting their welfare checks," I said.

The Puerto Rican part did not bother Walter. What
did bother him was the word "poor." By looking out
his window, he could see the future. And the future
he saw involved too many people without enough
money to adequately support the Dodgers. He could
see there was no way the Dodgers were going to make
it in Brooklyn, at least at Ebbets Field.

We had won the pennant in 1956, yet our attendance barely passed one million, 1,028,000 to be
precise. In the past, we had drawn as many as 1.8

million customers. Ebbets Field had seats for about
30,000 fans, which meant we had dropped from a
high of 78 percent of capacity to 45 percent.

Had the Braves not moved from Boston to Milwaukee, the Dodgers probably would still be in Brooklyn,
with a new stadium, of course. But when the Braves
relocated, their attendance soared, and we could not
compete financially. We would have had to sell out
virtually every night to make enough money to compete with the Braves. They were outdrawing us two
to one, despite the fact we had won four pennants in
five years. Walter feared that the Braves were stock-
piling money to be used against us to sign players.

The Dodgers weren't losing money in Brooklyn. We
always turned a profit, which, in those days, was all
you asked. No one was in baseball to reap a fortune.

The outlook was bleak. Ebbets Field was so run-
down the place had been on the verge of being
condemned several times. Walter had no choice. He
had to move the club somewhere. He wanted to stay
in Brooklyn, and to this day no one can convince me
otherwise. His roots were there, his family was there.

Walter, in fact, envisioned a domed stadium, long
before the Astrodome in Houston was built. He was
talking to architects about the feasibility of such a
stadium. We all thought he was nuts. One day, he
even had Eddie Roebuck, a proficient fungo hitter,
hit fungos straight up, to see how high the roof of a
domed stadium would have to be.

He even had a site chosen. He wanted to build it
right over the Long Island railroad tracks at Atlantic
and Flatbush avenues, in Brooklyn, equidistant from
Manhattan and Long Island. Three different rail-
roads and subway trains came through there. He
envisioned people from all parts of New York City
and Long Island attending Dodger games.

At one point, Walter thought he had the politicians

persuaded to build a stadium there, but they rejected
the idea at the last minute. The president of Queens
wanted to build a stadium in Flushing Meadow
(where Shea Stadium eventually was built), so he
asked Walter if he'd be interested in moving there.
The site was close to the booming suburbs on Long
Island.

Walter decided the rent they were asking was too
much. In retrospect, had they proposed the same
lease they eventually gave the Mets, Walter might
have taken it. The Mets received a small percentage
of the parking and all the concessions for every event
at the stadium, including football games, and in
return paid only a modest rental fee.

Another drawback to the Flushing Meadow site
was that it was not in Brooklyn. If the Dodgers
weren't playing in Brooklyn, how could they be the
Brooklyn Dodgers? Walter felt that if they had to
move from Brooklyn, it didn't really matter where
they went, whether it was Jersey City, where the
Dodgers had played some games, or Los Angeles.
Either way, they would no longer be the Brooklyn
Dodgers.

Throughout all this, no one thought Walter was
serious about moving. They suspected he was bluffing, the same way everyone in Los Angeles thought
Jack Kent Cooke was bluffing when he threatened to
build his own arena and move his basketball Lakers
and hockey Kings there; and everyone thought Carroll Rosenbloom was bluffing when he threatened to
move the Rams from the Coliseum to Anaheim
Stadium.

When people in New York realized O'Malley was
not bluffing, they formed a sports authority headed
by Robert Moses, the parks commissioner at the time.
It was all talk and no action, though. Too many people
got involved, even Nelson Rockefeller, who said he

was going to loan Walter some money to build his own stadium. We still don't know what Rockefeller's intentions really were, but Mayor Robert Wagner was quoted as saying it was merely a political front, that he did not plan to do anything. Wagner didn't do anything, either.

O'Malley intended to move somewhere, anywhere, and he was being wooed by the city of Los Angeles. Hank Greenberg and Bill Veeck had previously tried to put an expansion team there, but the league turned them down. Had Hank gone into it alone, he might have gotten it. But Veeck and Greenberg together were unable to garner enough votes.

A group of top political figures from California went to Vero Beach to make their pitch to O'Malley in February of 1957. It was their intention to build a stadium for Walter, who said no, "you just get us a piece of property and we'll build our own stadium." He did not want to have the city as his landlord.

In May of 1957, the group asked him to have a look at some property. From a helicopter he got his first look at Chavez Ravine and knew immediately the potential value of such property. Chavez Ravine is closer to city hall in Los Angeles than Central Park is to 42nd Street at Times Square in New York. It would be like building a stadium in Central Park.

One other site was being considered, down the street from the Forum in Inglewood. But it wasn't viable property for two reasons. First, it was next to a cemetery. Second, the city did not own the land. Walter would have had to buy it from a private party.

By this time the Giants had already decided they were going to leave New York. Owner Horace Stoneham was going to take them to Minneapolis, where the Giants had operated a successful minor league franchise.

I think Walter's hardest job was talking Horace out

of moving to Minnesota. The Giants owned a lot of property in Minnesota, and Horace liked the state. But Walter had to convince Horace that moving to San Francisco would be a better move, since it would allow the Dodgers-Giants rivalry to flourish as never before.

Meanwhile, Walter had sold Ebbets Field for $4 million, with the understanding that the Dodgers could play there through the 1959 season if need be; he also sold the Montreal ballpark for $1 million.

And then he pulled perhaps his greatest coup, next to acquiring the land at Chavez Ravine.

At a winter baseball dinner in 1957, Walter slipped a note to Phil Wrigley, who owned the Cubs, Catalina Island off the coast of Los Angeles, the Los Angeles Angels of the Pacific Coast League, and the ballpark those Angels played in, Wrigley Field.

Walter knew that Mr. Wrigley was irked at the city of Los Angeles, which wanted to annex Catalina Island. Walter's note that night to Mr. Wrigley—which, incidentally, was meant as nothing more than a gag—said, "I understand you want to get out of Los Angeles. We'll trade you our Fort Worth club for your Los Angeles club."

Mr. Wrigley shot a note back to Walter: "My son-in-law will be in to see you tomorrow morning." Wrigley's son-in-law, Bill Haganah, was the president of the Cubs.

The deal was consummated the next day. We received Wrigley Field and the Los Angeles Angels, and they got the Fort Worth club and the ballpark there.

Needless to say, it was not one of the better deals Mr. Wrigley ever made, since the Fort Worth club wasn't worth that much, though it did get him out of Los Angeles. But had Mr. Wrigley still owned the PCL franchise in Los Angeles, he could have made it far more difficult for the Dodgers to move there. He could have held them up for a ransom.

By September, 1957, Walter had pretty much decided to move, and by then everyone else knew the Dodgers would be heading west. People would come to Ebbets Field and rip the urinals out of the men's rooms and take them home as souvenirs. I have no idea what they planned to do with them.

Everyone had something to say about it. A Judge Lebowitz of the Superior Court, who had been given a box of four season tickets every year, was speaking at a radio broadcasters' dinner in New York that I attended.

"How could Walter do this to me?" he said, beginning a tirade. "I've been going to those games for 14 years. I never missed a home game. How can he do this to me and to all the people in Brooklyn?

"I wish Walter would do one thing for me. I wish he'd let me buy that seat that I sat in every night for 14 years."

"Judge," I said to him afterward, "that would be the first time you ever bought a seat at Ebbets Field."

For packing up his club and moving to California, O'Malley was crucified by the often heartless New York press. But who could blame the writers? They were upset because they were losing a valuable perk. We were the only club that took newspapermen and their families to spring training for two months. If you lived in New York and were accustomed to an all-expense-paid two months in Florida in the wintertime, you'd be mad, too.

Walter was accused of leaving out of greed; people were saying that he saw the California gold, that he went prospecting. If he did, so be it. He was entitled. Walter had sold everything he owned to move to California. He even had to pay the Pacific Coast League $900,000 for the right to take over its most productive territory.

The PCL was strong in those days. Its president,
Leslie O'Connor, was a tough man. He was not about
to allow anyone to take any cities from his league
without paying a price. And he was opposed to our
move because he felt that one day the PCL would be
an entire major league by itself.

As it turned out, he was nearly right. Every PCL
city except Portland eventually got a major league
team: Seattle, Oakland, San Francisco, Los Angeles,
and San Diego all got franchises.

Walter's first order of business was to establish an
organization. Most of the people who worked for the
Dodgers were New York–bred. I had lived virtually
all of my 41 years in Scarsdale. Fresco Thompson
lived in the Bronx and Freeport for years. Lee Scott
was a native, too.

Walter O'Malley wanted everyone to be happy with
the move to California. He knew none of us wanted to
go, so he gave raises. Harold Parrott, then the ticket
director, received a $2,500 raise. Scott, the road
secretary, received a $4,000 raise. Nearly everyone
received a raise of some sort.

Instead of giving me a raise, Walter sold me the
two-acre parking lot at Ebbets Field. "I want you to
have something that will stick to your ribs," Walter
said, using his favorite phrase.

I was to buy it at book value, which was nil at the
time since it had already been written off. I agreed,
provided I could include Fresco Thompson in the
deal, too. We had to have Fresco in California, because he was the man who kept things upbeat, kept
people smiling. So Fresco and I bought the parking
lot for $1 and planned to keep it two, three, or four
years until it appreciated.

It was a generous gesture on Walter's part, one that
obviously was not based on my previous management
of that lot when the Dodgers were still in Brooklyn. I

had hired a scorecard salesman by the name of Herman Levy to run the lot for me. For three weeks, we received complaints every day. Finally, someone came into the office with a picture showing a 2-by-4 through a car window.

I called Herman in and said, "What's going on? We've had nothing but trouble since you took over."

"Well, Buzzie, I didn't want the job in the first place," he said.

"Why not?"

"I never learned to drive."

I could only hope I would do a better job the second time around.

The Coliseum, our temporary home in Los Angeles, was not the best place to play baseball. It was a tough place to draw fans because there were so few good seats. No one was allowed to sell beer at the Coliseum in those days, which was an enormous hindrance to attendance. We received nothing for the concessions or parking. We were merely biding our time.

There was a great rumor circulating that the Coliseum Commission had asked Walter what he would need as compensation for the concessions. He allegedly told them that since we played a 154-game schedule, the concession revenue for half the games would be fair. Walter supposedly had the Dodgers keeping the concession money for the 77 games they played in the Coliseum, failing to tell the Coliseum Commission that its half of the games were all on the road.

This was only a story and it wasn't true, which is too bad. But if anyone could have pulled it off, Walter was the man.

In fact, resources were at a minimum when we moved. I remember going into Walter's office when

we first got to Los Angeles. He was sitting with his
head in his hands, wondering where he was going to
get the next installment to start the stadium. He just
didn't have the money.

Then there was the infamous left-field screen at the
Coliseum, which we had to take down at our expense
four or five times a year for football games.

"Why don't we find out how much those tickets cost
for the football games," I suggested. "Maybe it would
be cheaper to buy them, and then we could keep the
screen up."

That wasn't the answer.

"Let's find out how much it would cost to take the
screen down and put it back up," Walter said.

We asked one of the Coliseum groundskeepers to
find out the cost of taking the screen down for football
games, then putting it back up. The groundskeeper
told Walter it cost $4,562.77.

"How'd you find out?" Walter asked.

"We tried it last night."

That went over big.

The Dodgers were not a hard sell in Los Angeles.
Even before we left Brooklyn we began to sell season
tickets. So many checks came in we actually had
people picking up money with shovels.

Our debut in the Coliseum was inauspicious, to say
the least. Red Patterson had been in charge of pregame ceremonies, and when he was in charge of
anything, we had to do it his way or else trouble
would follow.

On opening night, moments before the game was to
begin, I looked down, and he was arguing with
someone. Later, I asked him what happened.

"A guy out there was giving me a hard time about

leaving the field," Red said, "until he told me who he was."

"Who was he?"

"Governor Knight."

Patterson had thrown the governor of California off the field.

We really had no choice but to play at the Coliseum. Wrigley Field was simply too small. We drew 1.8 million our first year in the Coliseum, and even had we sold out every game at Wrigley Field, we could not have reached that figure. Also, Walter was leery of playing in Wrigley Field for fear that people would associate a minor-league park with a minor-league operation. He wanted to avoid that kind of atmosphere. Walter figured that if we played in Wrigley Field, we'd get the old clientele, too. He wanted new fans.

One of the few regrets I have is that Roy Campanella never had a chance to play in the Coliseum. Oh, what he would have done to that left-field screen, just 251 feet down the line. He might have hit 100 home runs. He had hit so many long fly balls to left field in Ebbets Field, fly balls that would have been homers in the Coliseum.

But shortly before Christmas of 1957, Campanella was involved in the car accident that would leave him paralyzed for life. I will never forget that day.

Campy would eventually benefit in another way, however, from the Dodgers' playing in the Coliseum. On May 7, 1959, we staged an exhibition game against the Yankees for Campy's benefit, and we drew 93,103 fans, at the time the largest crowd ever to witness a major league baseball game.

Our share of the gate was $87,500, of which $50,000 went to Campy. We tried to convince the Yankees to give Campy a portion of their share of the gate too, but they refused. I thought maybe they'd give him $2,500 or $5,000. They laughed at me. They didn't give him 15 cents.

Walter fell in love with Chavez Ravine, and he was convinced that it was the perfect place to build Dodger Stadium, assuming an engineer could devise a method to deal with the inconsistent terrain. He traded Wrigley Field for the property, which, in retrospect, was like buying Manhattan Island from the Indians for $24. It was the kind of deal of which legends are built.

In addition to his acquiring the property for next to nothing, Walter also convinced the city to build the access roads leading up to the stadium. This was worth another $3 million to O'Malley. However, it was immediately subject to a large property tax.

It wasn't quite that easy, to be honest. Once we were in Los Angeles, we realized the city could not automatically produce what it had promised. We thought acquiring Chavez Ravine was a finished deal, but it wasn't. Because public land was involved, the people had to vote on whether we'd get it.

Still, we thought little about it. We assumed everyone in Los Angeles wanted major league baseball. We soon discovered otherwise. I guess we forgot that not everyone cares about baseball. The attitude many people had was that the Dodgers would take money out of their pockets, that instead of buying hot dogs at the grocery market, for instance, people might buy them at the ballpark.

Many people opposed our getting the land. And as the date on which the referendum would be put to a vote drew nearer, we became quite concerned.

At one point, we began to explore alternate sites. Some people from Quartz Hill, out in the desert about an hour north of Los Angeles, wanted us to build a stadium there. "No smog, no politics," they said. No fans, either, we said.

We decided to take a look at the Rose Bowl in Pasadena, to see if it could be structured to accommodate a baseball game. One foggy morning I went with Red Patterson, the Dodgers' public relations director, to make the secret investigation. No one could know. We feared if word got out that we were looking at the Rose Bowl in Pasadena, our chances in Los Angeles might be jeopardized.

"Now, Red, don't forget," I said, "don't tell anybody who we are. Just say we're looking at the Rose Bowl as a possible site for a concert or something."

We took a tape measure, and I stood where home plate would be, and Red, pulling the tape measure, walked out to where the right-field fence would be.

Suddenly, he shouts at me, "Hey, Buzzie, it's 352 feet to right field!"

So much for secrecy. All the workers at the Rose Bowl heard him.

"Red, come here," I said.

"What, I didn't say anything."

"Red, how many people named Buzzie are there in this world who are in the Rose Bowl this morning and care how far it is from home plate to right field?"

The referendum was too close for comfort. No one knows what might have happened to the Dodgers had the vote not gone in our favor. I think we were saved by the power of television.

On the Sunday before the vote, we staged a telethon. Several movie personalities went on the air for us and pleaded for the people's support, explaining to them how much the Dodgers would mean to the city of Los Angeles.

The man who may ultimately have been responsible for our victory was Ronald Reagan, then presi-

dent of the Screen Actors Guild, who made a con-
certed plea on our behalf.

We also pulled a public relations coup by trading
with Detroit for Steve Bilko, who as a minor-league
star in Los Angeles had been one of the most popular
players ever to play in the town.

Nevertheless, on the day of the vote, we were
uncertain of the outcome until about midnight. It was
so close the thought had entered my mind that maybe
I shouldn't have sold my home back in Scarsdale. As
it was, we probably would not have won the referendum without the telethon. But we did finally win.

What we actually won was a junkpile that would
eventually be transformed into a gold mine. Chavez
Ravine was landfill, a dump at one time. To build a
ballpark there was a remarkable feat, and we were
fortunate to have hired a brilliant engineer named
Captain Emil Praeger, who recognized the site's
potential right away.

Once we got the land, it still wasn't ours entirely. A
family had a little house and a store right where
second base is today. Their plot was valued at $6,000,
but it cost Walter $150,000 to buy them out.

We had nowhere to go but up.

8

Wills: Go Go Go

It is a tragedy, really. Baseball owes a debt of gratitude to Maury Wills, yet he may never be allowed to collect it.

It is not an exaggeration to say that Maury Wills changed the way baseball is played in much the same manner Babe Ruth changed it. The Babe introduced power to the game, forever changing the emphasis. Wills re-introduced speed.

Power, of course, is still important, but it is one-dimensional. It contributes only on offense. Speed, on the other hand, is a quality useful both offensively and defensively. And Wills was responsible for putting it back into the game.

He was electrifying in his prime, in the early sixties, when the Dodgers won with speed and pitching. Dodger Stadium crowds chanted, "Go, go, go," and Wills was gone, often stealing the base that would position him to score the lone run of the game.

Maury Wills began a trend for a new kind of baseball, and the Dodgers played it better than anyone. When Sandy Koufax pitched his third career no-hitter, Don Drysdale, who was not in attendance, asked, "Yeah, but did he win?" The Dodgers did not score much in those days. They had to manufacture runs, and runs are manufactured with speed.

Wills always played with the idea that one day he would become a major league manager. When his chance finally came with the Seattle Mariners in 1980, he announced that he was as prepared for the assignment as anyone ever was. But he was wrong, in a tragic way.

I suspect that some of Maury's problems stemmed from his desire to be the best, as well as his over-whelming knowledge of the game. This may sound silly, but Maury Wills reminded me at times of Frankie Frisch. Frisch played the game as well as anyone ever did but his record as a manager was mediocre.

Why? Because he thought that every player he managed should be a Frisch. Of course, if that were the case, there'd be no need to have a manager. The same went for Maury. He expected his players to have the same talent, drive, and dedication to the game that he had. But again, if you had nine Maury Wills on a club, you'd have no need for a manager.

It took Maury a long time to make it to the big leagues, but once he made it in 1959, things came easy for him. In fact, things came too easy for him. He was one of Walter Alston's favorites, he was on Alston's All-Star team. But had he followed Alston's theory about managing, Maury might still be active in baseball today. Walter always delegated authority to his coaches. Maury, on the other hand, insisted on doing everything himself. The job is too much for one man; how could Maury handle the pitching, fielding, and baserunning all by himself?

As a result, Maury's managing technique led to a brief career as a skipper, which is a shame when you consider his outstanding career as a player, and his apparent love and knowledge of the game.

In retrospect, I'm certain Wills had problems off the field that affected the way he went about his job. For instance, the Mariners were playing the Padres in Yuma in the spring of 1981; the next day they were to play the Angels in Palm Springs. Wills left the game with San Diego in the fifth inning to fly to Los Angeles for personal reasons. To me, that in itself would be grounds for firing a manager. You simply cannot do things like that. Imagine what kind of an example it sets for the players.

In the very first series of the 1981 season, the Mariners were playing the Angels in the Kingdome. The score was tied in the top of the ninth inning and Rod Carew was on third base. On the first couple of pitches, Carew feigned breaking toward the plate. Oblivious, Wills did not instruct his pitcher to work from a stretch. The pitcher wound up again, Carew stole home, and the Angels had a one-run victory. If nothing else, Wills, the most dominant base stealer of his era, should have known when a pitcher must hold a runner on base.

In Maury's case, it was never a matter of not knowing, but rather a matter of trying to do too many things. His knowledge of the game was so complete; but his potential as a manager was limited by his desire to do everything himself.

I don't think he'll ever get another chance to manage a major-league team, which is too bad. He can only point a finger at himself, though. Not only did he botch his opportunity in Seattle, he went there with his reputation already tainted.

When I was with the Padres, I received a call from Bob Lurie, the owner of the Giants. Bob wanted to

know what I thought of Wills as a managerial candidate. At the time, they were considering Wills and
Joey Amalfitano, and Joey had turned them down.

I told Bob I thought Maury possibly had the mak-
ings of a good manager, but that it would behoove
him to manage a Class AAA club first, to gain some
experience. The question wasn't his knowledge of the
game, but whether he could handle people. Wills, of
course, dismissed the notion that he needed experience. In his mind, he was ready for the major leagues.

Lurie asked if I would act as an intermediary by
arranging a meeting between Maury and the Giants.
I called Maury to explain the situation.

"Now look, Maury, what is the one thing you want
to do most in the world?" I said.

"I want to manage a big-league ball club," he said.

"It looks like you've got your chance," I said. "The
Giants called me and asked if I'd arrange a meeting
between you and Mr. Lurie and the other people in
San Francisco.

"This is your big opportunity," I continued, talking
to him like a father to his son. "Don't let money
interfere with your taking the job. If it's money you
want, don't take the job."

"Oh, no," he said. "Money doesn't mean anything. I
want that opportunity."

"That's what I wanted to hear you say. You want
the opportunity to manage a big-league club."

"They're not going to give me a minor-league
salary, are they?" he asked.

"No. They'll treat you just like they treat everybody
else. They'll be fair."

"You know I've got a job with NBC."

"Yes, but you're not making a whole lot of money.
And besides, you don't really have a job. They haven't
renewed your contract for next year. But please don't
let money interfere with your taking this job."

"I promise you I won't let money interfere," he said.

I called Lurie and said, "I think you've got yourself a manager, if you want him. Don't go overboard on the salary, but be fair with him, and I don't think you'll have a problem."

The next afternoon, Lurie phoned me and said, "What the hell's the matter with you?"

"What are you talking about?"

"You apparently don't know that young man very well," Bob said. "The first thing he wanted to know was how long his contract was going to be and how much money was in it. He said he had to have so much money, the same amount that Frank Robinson got for managing."

"What?" I said, incredulously. "How much is the difference?"

"Ten thousand dollars. But it wasn't the ten thousand we were opposed to, it was his attitude we were disturbed with."

I called Maury to find out what had happened. "Maury," I said, "I thought you and I agreed you weren't going to talk about money."

"Well, they didn't want to give me what I thought I deserve. If I can't get what I want, then that means they don't want me."

The next managerial job for which Wills was a candidate was with Seattle. Danny Kaye, a part owner of the club, called to inform me the Mariners were considering Wills.

"I'm disturbed about him, because of the problem you told me he had with the Giants," Danny said.

"I think that's behind him now," I said. "He needs a job now. It's not the same situation. He had a job to fall back on then."

Despite Danny's apprehensions, the Mariners hired Wills. He did not even last one full season.

I don't think his problems as a manager had

anything to do with his knowledge of the game. Wills knows baseball. He had to teach himself how to hit. He made himself a quality base runner. He made himself a good fielder. He faced all the hardships in baseball, but he overcame them.

One problem was that he did not understand human nature. He is not a born leader. He never communicated particularly well with his teammates. Had he done so, he might be managing today.

Wills's prime as a player was delayed by a lengthy minor-league career. His first spring training camp was in 1951, but he did not reach the major leagues until 1959, at the age of 26.

The Dodgers originally were interested in Wills as a pitcher. But at the tryout camp from which he was signed, Maury noticed a shortage of infielders. So he asked the camp organizer whether he could try out as a second baseman or a shortstop. He impressed the scouts, and was signed for $500.

He wasn't *that* impressive, though, to be honest about it. No one really took a second look at him. He did a fairly good job wherever he was sent, but he was never spectacular. Nor did he figure in the Dodgers' plans. I once made the statement that had someone offered me $11 and a bag of potato chips for Maury's contract, I'd have sold him.

The heir apparent to Pee Wee Reese at shortstop was Don Zimmer, and had Zimmer not broken his toe in 1959, the world might never have heard of Maury Wills. Zimmer had waited a long time for Pee Wee to retire, and when his chance finally came, an injury felled him.

Zimmer would not tell anyone he was injured, but it was immediately apparent that his range was cut in half. Then someone noticed that the leather of Zimmer's baseball shoe had been cut away to provide freedom for his toe.

Wills, meanwhile, had been sold to Detroit for
$40,000 on a conditional basis. The Tigers took him to
spring training and he played fairly well in Florida.
We sent a scout to the Tigers' camp to make sure
Wills was given an adequate opportunity.

At first we were certain the Tigers would keep
him, but they called to say they didn't think he was
worth $40,000. They were trying to depreciate his
value by claiming he would not make their team.

"We'll give you $20,000 for him, but we're going to
send him to Seattle (of the Pacific Coast League),"
they said. Every major league club, incidentally,
allowed him to go unclaimed through waivers.

"Wait a minute," I said. "If I agree to the $20,000,
you'll send him to Seattle and bring him back the
next day to save yourself $20,000. It's $40,000 or
nothing."

They declined, and Wills was back in our minor-
league system—until Zimmer broke his toe. Wills
was recalled on the recommendation of Bobby Bragan, who stood alone in his assessment of Wills. He
saw Maury as a star. Bragan, in fact, was the man
who made Wills a switch hitter, and thus, ultimately,
an All-Star.

Wills was not an immediate sensation. After
Maury had played with the Dodgers a couple of days,
Pee Wee came over to me and said, "Buzzie, you made
your first mistake." Three weeks later, Reese had
changed his tune. "Well, I guess I made the mistake,"
Pee Wee said.

Wills batted .260 in 83 games for our 1959 world
championship team. The following year he hit .295
with 50 stolen bases, and his potential was beginning
to show. Then in 1962, Wills had a phenomenal year:
he played in all 165 games, batted .299 with 208 hits
and 130 runs scored, and broke Ty Cobb's record for
stolen bases in a season with 104.

Based on that one season alone, 100 stolen bases became the standard by which runners would be measured, in the same way that 200 hits in a season is the standard by which great hitters are measured. Every swift youngster I had with the Dodgers or the San Diego Padres wanted to wear Wills's number 30. Maury had revolutionized the game.

Wills was a loner, not the sort of man who easily becomes a leader. He did his job on the field, then he'd leave and you wouldn't see him again until the next day. I think he came to the office once, when he was mad at Walter Alston.

Maury had fits of moodiness, too. He was given to brooding if he wasn't made to feel appreciated. Criticizing him was the worst thing you could do to him. He would take it personally, and the next thing you knew, he would take himself out of the lineup with an injury that everyone suspected did not exist.

In an attempt to placate him and to keep him in the lineup, Walter Alston and I decided to make him the captain of the Dodgers, an assignment he took seriously.

Unfortunately, he alienated his teammates in the process. He resigned as captain after a disagreement with Alston involving a player who was put off by Maury's intensity. Wills had formed a committee of three players and himself to serve as a kangaroo court. Walter allowed him to do it. But the first thing the committee did was fine Willie Davis $100 for loafing. Walter thought the fine was exorbitant and overruled the committee.

Maury came straight to my office and told me where to stick the captaincy. In doing so he saved me the $500 we were paying him to be the captain. But once again he had failed to show good judgment.

The next day, incidentally, he again took himself

out of the lineup with an injury that Alston questioned in front of the team. One day later, Wills was playing again, and he asked Alston to re-instate him as captain. Alston did.

When the 1966 World Series concluded—we had been swept by the Baltimore Orioles—the club was going on a goodwill tour of Japan. Evit and I did not want to spend six weeks in Japan, so we decided instead to take a 15-day cruise of the Hawaiian Islands.

The day before we were to set sail, I got a call from Walter O'Malley. Wills had jumped the club in Japan without permission. O'Malley's instructions to me were to dump him.

"Not only did he embarrass the Dodgers," Walter said, "but he embarrassed the nation of Japan."

I wasn't about to let Wills ruin my vacation. Dealing with him could wait until we returned to Los Angeles. One night in Hawaii, Evit and I went to see the "Don Ho Show," and who do you think was on stage with Don Ho? A hint: He is a prolific banjo player as well as a banjo hitter who once stole 104 bases for the Dodgers. Goodbye. We were out of there.

When I returned to work, my first order of business was to deal Wills, which wasn't easy for two reasons. First, it wouldn't be easy to look Wills in the eye, since we had given Koufax, Drysdale, and Wes Parker permission to skip the Japan trip. Nevertheless, Wills had committed himself to going, then jumped the club in Osaka with the excuse that an injured right knee needed immediate attention. En route home, he stopped in Hawaii to perform in a nightclub and, to my knowledge, didn't see a doctor for this alleged injury until two weeks after he had left the club. He could play for Don Ho, but he couldn't play for the Dodgers?

Second, it was hard to trade him because Walter

had made it known that Wills had worn out his welcome in Los Angeles. Everyone tried to hold us up. No one was willing to give us what Maury was worth at the time.

Finally, the Pirates proposed a trade that was agreeable to both parties. They weren't happy with infielders Bob Bailey and Gene Michael, we weren't happy with shortstop Maury Wills. The trade was made, and Wills left the Dodgers after eight tumultuous years. And although his statistics would portray him as a winner, his conduct would portray him as an enigma, a puzzle that we could never solve. It would be too many years before Maury could earn the respect he deserved.

9

Twin Terrors: Koufax and Drysdale

They were frequently paired, like Ruth and Gehrig, Mantle and Maris. Involuntarily but invariably, such pairs were joined for performing at the same time in the same town with abilities that transcended mortality. Each could stand on his own, a superstar in his own right. But put two such stars together and they can illuminate history.

And so it was with Koufax and Drysdale. They were record setters and history makers, thrown together by fate, which ostensibly knew they belonged together. Koufax and Drysdale were the heart and soul of the Dodgers of the 1960s. Wills was important and Tommy Davis won two batting titles, but Sandy Koufax and Don Drysdale were the Dodgers.

They were smart, too. They were aware of their value to the team individually, but, parlayed, they knew their worth would increase dramatically.

So together they made one of their best pitches, off the field. In January of 1966, they threw us a curve ball. They formed their own union, of which they were the only members. In an effort to extract an exorbitant amount of money from Walter O'Malley's otherwise tightly sealed bank account, Sandy and Don decided to negotiate as one.

It wasn't a bad idea. The Dodgers had won National League pennants and World Series titles in 1963 and 1965, and is it any wonder? Koufax and Drysdale, half our starting rotation, would one day wind up as Hall of Famers.

When two pitchers of that caliber join forces in contract negotiations and threaten to hold out if their terms aren't met, it is indeed a crisis. Imagine what the Dodgers would do today if Fernando Valenzuela and Orel Hershiser pulled a similar ploy. The prospect of losing more than 40 victories can serve as a splendid negotiating tool.

In 1966, we were looking at a pair of pitchers threatening to abscond with 49 victories—Koufax had won 26 games, Drysdale 23, in 1965.

We had never negotiated in this manner before and were reluctant to start. Koufax and Drysdale intentionally walked, in what became the Great Holdout.

The scenario began in January, when I received a phone call from Don informing me that he and Sandy would be coming in to see me together. I had no idea what it was they wanted to talk about. At the time, I assumed it was about a charity function.

They came in that afternoon, and Don got right to the point.

"We want to talk about a contract," Don said. I had sent both of them contracts, but neither had returned his signed.

Don said, "We decided we should come in together and negotiate the same points and the same amount of money."

"I've never done this before, and I don't intend to start now," I said. "But I'll listen to you."

I didn't listen for long. They were seeking three-year contracts for $500,000 each. In 1965, Koufax had made $85,000 and Drysdale had made $80,000. My budget called for Sandy to receive a raise to $100,000 or so and Drysdale to get a raise to about $90,000.

"We can't do that," I said. "I'll talk to Walter O'Malley about it, but I know his position on multi-year contracts."

His position, of course, was that he did not believe in them. No one in baseball had a multiyear contract in those days, and Walter was adamantly opposed to making Koufax or Drysdale the first.

At our next meeting, they said they'd settle for $150,000 a year for three years, which was still two years too many and thousands too much.

Shortly before we were to leave for Vero Beach for spring training, Don, Sandy, and I met for the third time, and they were beginning to waver. They indicated they would settle for less than $150,000 each.

I told them I could give them about $195,000 between the two of them, but not in a package. I told Sandy that I intended to pay him more, but that if he cared to give some of his own money to Drysdale to equalize their salaries, that was his business.

They declined, and the Great Holdout officially began. So had spring training, sans Koufax and Drysdale, whom I maintain to this day we could have signed in a minute. But there wasn't any reason to sign them. The holdout was making headlines in every paper in the Los Angeles area every day. I explained this to Walter O'Malley, who as well as anyone understood the value of publicity.

"Walter, we can settle this in five minutes," I said, "but we'd lose all those headlines."

It was my contention that eight weeks of spring training wasn't necessary anyway, and that both of them could be ready in two weeks, if need be.

Walter played along with it brilliantly. He knew how to agitate the situation, by calling the boys at a propitious time—when they were out. He'd leave messages for them to call him, and they would religiously return the calls. Then, Walter would tell the reporters that the boys were getting anxious to come back, that they were calling every day.

Meanwhile, they threatened to go to Japan to pitch, which I found amusing. They could not pitch in Japan without our permission. At the time, baseball still had its reserve clause, and the Japanese leagues honored it.

They decided they'd try show business, even signing to appear in a movie. And on the night after they'd finally signed their baseball contracts, they appeared on a Bob Hope television special and did a tap dance routine in top hat and tails.

Too bad they hadn't gone on the show the day before they signed. I would have saved Walter O'Malley $50,000. They were awful. The Dodgers should have won an Oscar for preventing Koufax and Drysdale from making a movie.

At no time were there any harsh words from either party. It never got ugly. It did get troublesome, however, particularly when we got within two weeks of the season opener. I was concerned that with so little time to train, they might try to rush and get hurt in the process.

Drysdale, I knew, worked out almost every day, but Sandy did not. Sandy already had arthritis by that time, and he did not care to aggravate it by throwing a baseball needlessly.

About two weeks before the season opened, I had a call in Vero Beach from Chuck Connors, who said, "Buzzie, these two fellows want to sign. It's just a matter of pride."

"Well, Chuck," I said, "it's a matter of pride for

both sides. I don't think money is a problem, though."

"Why don't you come on out to Los Angeles and I'll arrange a meeting."

I agreed. Connors and I were close and he was close to both Drysdale and Koufax. He took it upon himself to get involved because he knew how stubborn both Drysdale and I could be. He was interested, primarily from a fan's standpoint, in seeing this settled. He didn't want it prolonged any more than we did.

Connors arranged the meeting at a restaurant near the stadium. And indeed money was not a problem. We settled our differences quickly and went up to Dodger Stadium to make out the contracts and have them signed.

We got to my office and I asked Edna Ward, my secretary, to make out two contracts, one for $125,000 for Koufax and one for $110,000 for Drysdale.

"Wait a minute," Sandy said. "We decided we should get the same salary."

"Oh, OK," I said. "Edna, make out two of them for $117,500."

"Oh, no, that's OK, Buzzie. Let it go." He assumed I was going to make out both contracts for $125,000. All along, I insisted that Koufax be paid more. We paid him for winning games and setting records and we paid Drysdale for winning games. Koufax was more of an attraction and was worth more.

They joined the club in Arizona. Drysdale, I think, overworked himself. He had been working out every day at home, and he did not need to push himself. I think he got tired, which was reflected in his 13–16 season.

Sandy, meanwhile, worked steadily, and he had his greatest season. He was 27–9 with a 1.73 earned run average, and he personally punctured the myth that eight weeks of spring training is necessary to prepare for the opening of the season.

Between them they won 40 games, and the Dodgers again won the National League pennant. Aiding our effort in no small part was rookie pitcher Don Sutton, who had made the club only because Koufax and Drysdale had held out. Because they were absent from spring training, Sutton received an opportunity to display his skills. He won 12 games that year and went on to a brilliant career that includes more than 300 wins.

I've often wondered how much Koufax and Drysdale would command if they were playing today and came in together and asked for $2 million each. What would you do? Make them partners in the club?

The money we paid them in 1966 was substantial in those days. But we were proud of the fact we had two players earning $100,000 or more. We may have been the only club at the time to have two such salaries. Reluctantly, we had to admit to ourselves that their ploy worked. Koufax had gotten a $40,000 raise, Drysdale a $30,000 raise. Had they negotiated alone, neither would have gotten that much.

As it was, they unknowingly took money out of the pockets of the 23 other players. We had budgeted $100,000 for salary increases for the entire club, and when Koufax and Drysdale took $70,000 of that, it left just $30,000 in raises for the rest of the team.

In an article I wrote for *Sports Illustrated* in 1967, I proved to be a prophet of sorts. Koufax had said that, after I refused to negotiate through their agent, Bill Hayes, I gave in and called him, to which I wrote:

"Well, if I did that, I opened the door to more trouble than baseball ever dreamed in its worst nightmares. If I gave in and began negotiating baseball contracts through an agent, then I set a precedent that's going to bring awful pain to general managers for years to come, because every salary negotiation with every humpty-dumpty fourth-string catcher is going to run into months of dickering."

Sadly, I turned out to be right.

Ironically, money was not especially important to Koufax. He made $125,000 in 1966 and won 27 games. How much could he have gotten in 1967? We'll never know, because he chose to retire.

Even when we first signed him, virtually sight unseen out of the University of Cincinnati, he settled for less money from us in order to honor his word. His word wasn't in writing, either, which tells you something about the man's character.

We signed Sandy partly because he was a pretty fair basketball player. Most of us in the organization never actually saw Sandy pitch before the club signed him. The one day we went out to see him, the game was rained out. Al Campanis, a scout at the time, had seen him pitch, and Al recommended him highly because of his athletic ability.

Sandy's stepfather, Irving Koufax (Sandy had taken his last name), came in to see me in June to discuss a contract, and he said he'd like to have a $14,000 bonus for Sandy. I agreed. But by giving him that much, we had to keep him on the major league roster for two years.

At the time, we had no room on our roster, and Sandy wasn't going to play that year anyway. I was honest with them. I explained that at the end of the year, we were going to sell Preacher Roe and Billy Cox to Baltimore, and then we'd have room to sign Sandy and put him on the roster.

They agreed to wait until October to sign with us, we shook hands, and Mr. Koufax left. On the way out, he ran into Ed McCarrick, who was employed by the Pittsburgh Pirates. Ed came into my office and said he just saw Mr. Koufax.

"To be honest with you," Ed said, "Mr. Rickey told me to offer him $5,000 more than you offered him."

"That's your privilege," I said.

"He turned us down."

"I figured he would."

A month later, John Quinn of the Milwaukee Braves offered him about twice as much as we had offered, and he turned them down, too. All we had was a handshake at the time. We did not have a contract. Yet, the handshake was as good as a contract to Sandy and his stepfather. It was then and there I figured Sandy had to be a great man.

In 1955, Koufax was raw talent. His aim was as bad as his arm was good. Some of the veteran players refused to take batting practice off him because he was so wild.

It took a great deal of patience on the club's part. Sandy had the determination to make himself a quality pitcher, but he also had a manager willing to wait. Had Charley Dressen been managing the Dodgers instead of Walter Alston, I wonder whether Koufax would ever have matured into the pitcher be became. Dressen did not have the patience Alston did.

Once Sandy learned how to pitch, he was almost unbeatable. As a youngster, he was afraid to lose, which later became an asset. Once he harnessed his control, he did not lose very often.

Sandy was the best left-handed pitcher in history, as far as I'm concerned. People say that Lefty Grove was a great pitcher, and I'm sure he was. Carl Hubbell was a great left-hander, too. But people who say Grove or Hubbell or anyone else was a better left-hander must not have seen Koufax in his prime. Sandy was power and curve, power and curve, and he controlled it.

From 1963 through 1966, Koufax won 97 games

and lost just 27, for an average record of 24–6. He had
31 shutouts in those four years. Then he retired,
unexpectedly, at 30, with his most substantial earning and pitching years ahead of him.

Sandy Koufax amazed me three times in my life.
The first was when he and his dad honored the oral
agreement to sign with the Dodgers. The second time
was when he pitched his fourth no-hitter, a perfect
game against the Cubs on September 9, 1965. The
third time was when he elected to retire.

It wasn't the pain. As Roberto Clemente once said,
"All I know about Sandy's arthritis is that it must
come after the game is over. Nobody could pitch the
way Koufax does with something bothering him."

Koufax chose to retire because of the damage he
might have done to his arm had he continued pitching. He did not want to spend his retirement years
partially crippled.

Today, a pitcher would take the money first, then
he would not pitch, complaining of a sore arm. This is
what I found remarkable about Sandy. He could have
done that. He was entitled to another healthy raise.
Instead, he chose to quit.

Sandy was a man of principle. He would always do
what he thought right, regardless of the conse-
quences or what others might think of him. For
instance, Sandy was Jewish, and he refused to pitch
on Yom Kippur, a Jewish holiday that would sometimes fall during the World Series.

The 1965 World Series between the Dodgers and
the Minnesota Twins opened on Yom Kippur. Koufax
would not pitch. Instead, we used Don Drysdale in
the Series opener.

Drysdale had had only two days rest, and he wasn't
up to it: we lost. The next day, Koufax pitched with
two extra days rest and he was wild, and we lost
again. Had Koufax opened the Series, he probably

would have shut out the Twins. Then Drysdale would have started the second game with an adequate amount of rest, and he probably would have won. As it was, we won the third and fourth games, which conceivably could have given us a sweep.

I've always said the fact Koufax would not pitch on Yom Kippur made us a lot of money, perhaps $1 million. Had he pitched the first game of the '65 Series, we might have swept the Twins in four straight. Instead, it took us seven games, which considerably increased the size of everyone's coffers.

On the same subject, this conversation took place one year between Walter Alston and Danny Goodman, the Dodgers' concessionaire:

Walter: "When does Yom Kippur come this year?"

Goodman: "It comes on Tuesday, the opening day of the Series. But you've got no problem until Drysdale tells you he won't pitch on Yom Kippur, either."

Koufax, in my opinion, could have pitched several more years, and effectively, too. Whatever pain he had, he was able to pitch through it in 1965 and 1966, and undoubtedly he could have done the same in the ensuing years. But the risk involved was the deciding factor in his early retirement.

Unendurable pain ended Drysdale's career. Back then, it was simply said that a pitcher's arm went dead. In the seventies, doctors finally came up with a medical explanation. Those many dead arms were actually torn rotator cuffs.

A torn rotator cuff is what ended Drysdale's career prematurely, at age 32. It was unfortunate. But despite being deprived of four or five quality seasons, he still was elected to baseball's Hall of Fame.

Drysdale was one of my favorite men in baseball. He was one of those who would come to the office frequently, just to sit and talk baseball. In fact, when

I left the Dodgers, he presented me with a diamond money clip.

Once on a road trip, he and Johnny Podres came to my room after a game for a nightcap. Drysdale had this habit of leaning back in his chair, with the front legs off the ground. This time he leaned too far and he fell back. His head missed the television set by inches.

All I could envision was the next day's headline:

DRYSDALE DRUNK IN BAVASI'S ROOM, OUT SIX WEEKS

During spring training in Vero Beach in 1985, the Dodgers had a reunion of the 1955 club. I saw Sandy pitch on the side. So help me, if you didn't know it was Sandy Koufax, you'd think it was some 18-year-old kid. The motion was fluid, and the curveball was as sharp as it ever was.

Rumors circulated that he was considering a comeback. If he still had the reflexes necessary to protect himself from sharply hit balls, you'd be tempted to ask him to go out there and pitch.

He was 49 at the time.

10

Sweet Lou to Dodger Blue

Sweet Lou was Lou Johnson, the eccentric Dodger outfielder in the sixties. He was a free spirit, or, to use a definition preferred in baseball circles, a flake. He was, too, a treat to employ, and I'll tell you more about him in a minute.

The Dodger coup was the Class of '68, undoubtedly the best draft a club has ever enjoyed. It produced, among others, Steve Garvey, Ron Cey, Davey Lopes, Bobby Valentine, Bill Buckner, Joe Ferguson, Tom Paciorek, Doyle Alexander, and Geoff Zahn.

Lou Johnson and the Class of '68 were among the men and the stories contained within the boundaries of my Los Angeles years, from 1958 to 1968. The boundaries, themselves, are another story.

This was an era that began tragically for one man and ended sadly for another. I was the man for whom it ended sadly, for 1968 was the year in which I left the Dodgers. I had worked for the club for 30 years, and leaving was traumatic.

The tragic part was, of course, the auto accident in late 1957 that left Roy Campanella paralyzed for life. To say the least, it was a foreboding way to begin our stay in Los Angeles. That day, I went to New York and sat by Campy's bedside for about a week. He was special to me.

When he had come into baseball, he was a young man without a chip on his shoulder. He had no animosity toward anyone, he just enjoyed himself. I'll always have a special place in my heart for Campy.

The accident set in motion a year all of us would like to forget, and had some of us wishing we could return to Brooklyn. The Dodgers finished seventh in 1958. Relocating to California was part of the shock, and so was Campy's accident. He added a dimension beyond his ability to play the game. His personality was an intangible. He made the game enjoyable for others, and he would be missed.

John Roseboro took over for Campy, and though he did a commendable job, it wasn't quite enough. Our '58 club wasn't the worst, but it never did put it all together. The stars who shined in Brooklyn were beyond their primes in Los Angeles. We were an embarrassment that year.

The last day of the season was horrible. We lost when pitcher Roger Craig, attempting to field a bunt with his bare hand instead of his glove, dropped the ball. Had we won, we'd have finished fifth.

"You dumb SOB," I said to Craig afterward. "How much did you pay for that glove of yours?"

"Twenty-five dollars," he said.

"Why don't you use it?"

I was mad. Charley Dressen, coaching for us then, told the players to put their uniforms in a box to be sent to Vero Beach.

"Dammit, put all of them in," I said. "Even though some of you aren't going to need them in Vero Beach, because you won't be there."

Steaming, I went into another room, where a huge postgame spread of chicken, potato salad, and cole slaw sat on a big table. When Elmer Valo and Duke Snider each took a piece of chicken, I said, "If you take a bite of that chicken, we're going to work out tomorrow."

I was really mad. I asked our clubhouse attendant, Charlie DiGiovanni, what the spread was for.

"To celebrate the last game of the season," he said.

I turned the table upside down and walked out.

Two months later, Charlie came in to see me. "Remember that table you turned over? I picked up the chicken and put it in the trunk of my car," he said.

"Good."

"Yeah," he said, "but I forgot about it."

It cost him $42 to have the odor removed.

The beauty of baseball is that there is always a next year. And the next year for the Dodgers was a special one. The '59 team was not the best club with which I was ever associated, but it was my favorite club.

It was a patchwork club that won on guts and adhesive tape. Dr. Robert Kerlan, our team doctor, was probably our MVP. What the '59 Dodgers lacked in talent, they made up in heart. It was, unquestionably, the best managing job Walter Alston ever did.

With eight games left, the Dodgers and the Milwaukee Braves trailed the San Francisco Giants by two games, and the Giants were prematurely contemplating whether to host the World Series in Seals Stadium or to open the yet-to-be-finished Candlestick Park.

But the Giants finished third. The Dodgers and the Braves, led by Fred Haney, tied for the National League pennant, which came to Los Angeles for the first time by virtue of the Dodgers' two-game sweep in the best-of-three playoff with Milwaukee.

This was the year of the Moon Shot. Wally Moon, a left-handed hitter, mastered the art of lofting the ball over the left-field screen at the Coliseum. Moon hit 19 homers for us, most of them at the Coliseum.

The Coliseum paid off handsomely for the Dodgers in '59. We drew more than 90,000 for each of the three World Series games held there. And we won the World Series, four games to two, over the Chicago White Sox. It had taken the Brooklyn Dodgers 53 years to win their first World Series. It took the Los Angeles Dodgers just two years.

Two years later, I would receive an offer that I could not refuse, yet I did. At the 1961 World Series in New York, I was approached by Mr. Frank Stevens, a prominent concessionaire and a member of one of the finest families I have ever had the privilege of knowing.

Mr. Stevens called me into his office (under the stands in Yankee Stadium) and said, "We understand the National League is going to expand next year, and New York is going to get a club. The price is going to be about a million-eight, according to [National League president] Warren Giles. We don't want to get involved in running a baseball club. All we want is to operate the concessions."

Then he handed me a piece of paper. It was a check for $1.8 million.

"We want you to get the club," he said.

I was dumbfounded. "That's very nice of you," I said, but Walter O'Malley asked me to go with him to the west coast. He's been very kind. He's given me something that's going to stick to my ribs."

I explained to him about the parking lot Walter

had given me as an inducement to go to Los Angeles.

"I don't think it would be fair to Walter for me to back out now," I said.

On the spot, I turned the offer down. I never had any regrets, either. Evit and the boys had grown to like California, and Walter was a splendid man to work for.

Mr. Stevens and his brothers understood. They were quality people, who appreciated a man who kept his word. Every Christmas for 46 years, Evit and I have received a turkey from the Stevens family.

For the sake of the Los Angeles fans, the Dodgers unwillingly re-created the 1951 season, in which the Brooklyn team had lost an enormous lead to the Giants, then lost the National League pennant to them in the playoffs.

This time, 1962, we lost 10 of our last 13 games to fall into a tie with the Giants at the end of the regular season. The teams split the first two games of the best-of-three playoff, and the Dodgers took a 4-2 lead into the ninth inning of the third game. Four Giant runs later, San Francisco was in the World Series.

Then came 1963. The Dodgers won the pennant by six games and swept the Yankees in the World Series, winning four in a row.

About a week after the series, Evit and I were dining with the O'Malleys at Chasen's in Beverly Hills. I excused myself to go to the men's room and ran into Cary Grant, who was a great Dodger fan. Cary mentioned how happy Walter must be about beating the Yankees in four straight. I told Cary to go over and ask Walter that given his choice, would he rather the Dodgers lose in seven games than win in four. (The difference was about $1 million in revenue.) Later, I asked Cary what Walter's response was.

"Walter pleaded the fifth," Cary said. "He refused to answer on the grounds he might incriminate himself."

Tickets were at a premium for the '63 Series— everyone could have gotten rich scalping them. Baseball people took 25 percent of the tickets and season-ticket holders wanted another 80 percent. So we were at 105 percent before we even began distributing them.

A friend of mine, Benny Goffstein, the president of the Riviera Hotel in Las Vegas, offered me $250,000 in cash for 1,000 tickets. He had the $250,000 in a suitcase.

"Benny, they're only worth $7 apiece," I said.

"We're not going to sell them," he said. "We're going to give them to our high rollers."

"I can't do that, Benny. You get four tickets because you're a season customer. And you get four for being a Stadium Club member. That's eight tickets. That's all I can get you."

"You can't do any better than that?"

"I'd rather not."

About a week later, one of the girls from our auditing department went to Vegas, saw something suspicious, and apparently reported it to Walter O'Malley.

"Buzzie, did you give somebody by the name of Benny Goffstein a bunch of World Series tickets?" Walter asked.

"No, why?"

"He's giving them away over in Vegas, on television. Guess the right number and you win two tickets to the World Series. He's doing it twice a day."

I called Benny and asked if maybe he hadn't gone into our ticket office with the same proposal he had made to me. That might have been too great a temptation there.

"No, I wouldn't do that," Benny said. "You told me I had eight tickets."

"Where are you getting the tickets to give away?" I asked.

He started laughing. "How much did I offer you for the tickets?" he said.

"Two-hundred-fifty dollars each."

"All right. We're having a contest here, and when they win the tickets, they come in to claim them. I say, "OK, what do you want, the tickets or $500?" They take the $500 every time. So I use the same tickets over and over."

I had one other notable experience with World Series tickets, in 1966, when the Dodgers played the Baltimore Orioles. Lee MacPhail, Larry MacPhail's son, was the president of the Orioles.

Larry, my first boss with the Brooklyn Dodgers, came to town at the last minute with seven other people, and I assumed he would be the guest of his son, Lee. I was wrong. Lee called on behalf of his father and said he needed eight tickets.

"You know I don't have any tickets left," I said. "The only tickets left are in the last box along the right-field foul line. Why don't you put him in your box?"

"I've got my owners with me," Lee said.

I didn't know what to do. After pondering this dilemma for awhile, I came up with a solution. I called our groundskeeper and asked him to work the night before the Series opened.

"You know the 200 seats we have down the right-field line?" I asked, referring to temporary seats we installed for the World Series, in front of the permanent field-box seats. "I want you to reverse the numbers on them."

"What do you mean?" he asked.

"Well, they go from 1 to 200. I want you to make them go from 200 to 1."

The seats that remained had previously been down the right-field line. By reversing the numbers, seat No. 200 was right next to the dugout, which is where I put Larry MacPhail and his party. Some poor guy thought he had bought seats next to the dugout, only to discover they were down the right-field line.

Larry MacPhail, meanwhile, undoubtedly thought I'd saved those seats for him. I don't think he ever knew otherwise.

Over the years, Dodger Stadium was used for various concerts, notably those by the Beatles and Elton John. Concerts were not my area of expertise, however, as I discovered soon after the stadium had opened.

An agent called me, asking if I would consider booking his client to perform a concert at Dodger Stadium at a cost to us of $3,000.

"Who's your client?" I asked.

"Barbra Streisand."

I had no idea who Barbra Streisand was, and I declined the offer.

A year later, we had another chance to book Streisand. By then I knew quite well who she was, and I was anxious to book her, particularly at $3,000.

"What will it cost us?" I asked the agent.

"Sixty thousand dollars," he said.

Show business clearly was not my forte.

A man who became a close friend of mine in Los Angeles was Dr. Robert Kerlan, the noted orthopedic surgeon who was the Dodgers' team doctor for years. When the Dodgers were on the road, Dr. Kerlan and

Two of my heroes in 1951: Mel Ott (left) was the manager of Oakland's team in the Pacific Coast league, and Carl Hubbell (right) was the director of the New York Giants farm system. That's me in the middle, when I was vice president of the Brooklyn Dodgers.

Russ "Monk" Meyer, Jackie Robinson, me, and Clem Labine, all "Bums" from the fifties.

Fresco Thompson (left), me, and Walter O'Malley watch the city of Brooklyn celebrate the 1955 World Champion Dodgers.

A hug from Roy Campanella. The man on the left is Don Newcombe's father.

Walter Alston managed the Dodgers to seven pennants and four World Championships during his 23 years with the team.

Pee Wee Reese and Jackie Robinson stopped
by to sign autographs for my sons Peter
(standing) and Chris, and my wife Evit.

Maury Wills: he was a puzzle we could never solve.

Koufax and Drysdale: who could afford them today?

Two of my favorite people, my wife Evit and Walter Alston.

My home team (left to right): Bob owns the minor league
Everett Giants, Chris is the director of a federal Indian
program, Bill runs the Angels minor league operation, and
Peter is the former president of the Cleveland Indians.

They're winners in my book: Gene Autry and Red Patterson.

The 1955 Brooklyn Dodgers then . . .

... and at the thirty year rounion in 1985 at Vero Beach,

Now that I'm out of baseball, Evit and I can spend more time together.

I would travel to Del Mar during the racing season there.

Evit and I and Bob and his wife, Rachel, would stay at the Del Charro Hotel in nearby La Jolla. One night, we were going to have dinner in our rooms, and we all got into our pajamas and sat down to eat.

We had won our game that day, and the Giants were playing at home that evening.. At night, we could often get the Giants' broadcast on the radio. This time, we couldn't get it on our transistor.

"Bob," I said after dinner, "let's get in the car and go up to the top of the hill, and see if we can't get the game on the car radio."

Bob agreed. He drove us to this country lane atop a hill in La Jolla, and we parked. We were still in our pajamas. I had my head virtually in his lap to get my ear close enough to the radio in an attempt to find the game.

Suddenly, I looked up and there stood the biggest cop you ever saw. He was shining his flashlight on us and asked, "What are you doing?"

"You'll never believe this, officer, but I'm trying to get a baseball game on the radio," I said nervously.

"In your pajamas?"

I was envisioning the headlines in the paper the next day:

BAVASI, KERLAN IN SEX SCANDAL
UP IN WOODS

Fortunately, the policeman let us go.

In 1967, Bob and I decided to attend the World Series in Boston. Evit and Rachel chose to stay home, so Bob and I shared a room. It was about 1 A.M., and I was in bed reading.

"Bob," I said, "I hate to tell you this, but Evit tells me if I'm really tired, I have a tendency to snore."

"Oh, that's no problem," he said.

"I don't want to keep you awake."

"Here," he said, and he gave me two pills. "This will take care of it."

At breakfast the next morning, he asked, "How'd you sleep?"

"I didn't sleep a wink. I've been up all night. I finished the book. What did you give me?"

"Benzedrine."

"Benzedrine? That'll keep you awake."

"Yeah, but you didn't snore."

One time, at the Roosevelt Hotel in New York, Johnny Podres and Sandy Koufax had arm problems that required medical attention. Dr. Kerlan brought them to my suite and gave them both a shot.

About 2 P.M., the house detective came to see me in my room.

"I have to ask you some questions before I call the police," he said.

"About what?"

He had two hypodermic needles in his hand.

"What about them?" I said.

"Somebody appears to have been using drugs."

I laughed at him. "You silly ass," I said. "The doctor gave two of our players cortisone shots." The maid had found the empty syringes and turned them over to hotel security.

In 1965, I first encountered Sweet Lou Johnson. Tommy Davis, twice a National League batting champion, had broken his leg, so we summoned Johnson from our Spokane farm club to play left field for the Dodgers.

Spokane was playing in Seattle at the time, and we

gave Johnson a ticket on Northwest Airlines. What did he do? He returned the ticket for cash, then bought another ticket with a check. The check bounced. This was my introduction into the ethereal world of Lou Johnson, and what a character he was.

Still you couldn't get mad at him, though I tried. One day, I received a bill for $420 from a Milwaukee department store. It had Lou Johnson's name on it. I called him into my office.

"Lou, why the hell are you sending me a bill for $420 from a department store in Milwaukee?" I asked.

"Well, gee, Buzzie, I didn't have any money and I had to buy some clothes for my children."

"Is that right? How old are they?"

"One is four and one is six."

"Oh, and they both wear a 42-long, huh?" I said. The bill was for two suits, 42-long.

Another time, I received a call from a man at Westinghouse, who said, "Mr. Bavasi, I just sold an answering machine to one of your players." He was calling to verify that Lou was indeed employed by us.

"Which player?" I asked.

"Lou Johnson. He bought it on time. He's going to pay $50 a month."

"Fine," I said. "He can afford $50 a month. That's all right."

This was May. In August, the man called again.

"Mr. Bavasi," he said, "Lou Johnson hasn't made any payments whatsoever."

"What have you done about it?" I asked. "Call him up and tell him to send you your money."

"Mr. Bavasi, we call every day and all we get is his damn answering machine."

Walter O'Malley got mad at Lou once. On the Dodgers' 1966 tour of Japan, Lou bounced a check for

$300 through an American Express office there. When he returned, he knew we were mad at him.

"Oh, I wouldn't want to embarrass you or the club," he said, and he started to cry.

"Just go down and pay it back," I said.

He went down and paid it back, all right. He paid it back with another bad check.

Another favorite was outfielder Al Ferrara. He was always behind on his payments, whether taxes, rent, or anything. And he always had a gimmick. When he played in San Diego, he'd borrow from legitimate loan companies, to the tune of seven or eight thousand dollars. Then he'd forget to repay it, knowing I'd get him off the hook. Eventually, the loan companies would come to the ballclub, and I'd pay them 60 or 70 cents on the dollar. Finally, Al ran out of loan companies.

He was a character. Al was later traded to Cincinnati for Angel Bravo, and in his very first game, he went after a grounder, fell down, and the ball went through his legs. When reporters questioned him about the error, he replied, "Who do you think you got for Angel Bravo, Willie Mays?"

Al was romancing a pretty blonde, who had a bank account of $2,200. Soon thereafter, she didn't have a quarter. She did, however, have a ledger with all the bets Al had made on the horse races, as well as a record of all his poker losses.

She came in one day and told me how Al had lost all her savings. Then she told me something he had said to her eight-year-old daughter the night before.

I told her to bring him in to see me the next day. She brought him in and said to him, "Now tell him what you told my daughter two nights ago."

"What do you mean?" Al asked her.

"You told her to go piss in her hat."

"Don't talk that way in front of Buzzie," he scolded her.

I finally gave her a check for the $2,200 he owed her and told her to move somewhere else. They were separated for two days, then got back together, with my $2,200. To this day, I think it was a con job, but how could I get mad? Al was one of those players—it was hard to dislike him.

One year, Ferrara was to earn $20,000, and knowing him as I did, I was concerned that he wouldn't save enough money to get him through the winter.

"Al," I said, "you're making $20,000, but you're living like you're making $40,000. Here's what I'm going to do. I'm going to take $1,000 a month out of your salary and put it in a bank account in your name, so at the end of the season you'll have $6,000 saved."

To ensure he wouldn't spend the money prematurely, I arranged so he could not withdraw the money without my approval.

At the end of the season, I instructed the bank to let him have the money.

"There is no money," I was told.

"What?" I asked. "That's impossible. He couldn't withdraw the money without my approval."

On the first of every month, Ferrara had gone to the bank and borrowed $1,000 against the $1,000 we had deposited for him. He used it as collateral. When the season was over, he hadn't saved a penny.

When talking about characters, one of the great ones is Donald Davidson, for a long time the traveling secretary of the Braves and now an executive with the Houston Astros.

Davidson is not even four feet tall, though he stood 10 feet tall to those who knew him. The Dodgers were playing an exhibition game against the Braves one spring in Sarasota, Florida, the winter home of Barnum & Bailey Circus. The old man at the press gate had been there thirty years and he would not allow anyone to pass without a proper credential.

Someone told the man that a short person posing as the traveling secretary of the Braves would attempt to talk his way into the game, but that this short man was really with the circus. When Davidson arrived, the man would not allow him to enter. Finally, Davidson blew his top and a fight ensued. Davidson was on his toes, attempting to hit the man, but he could get no higher than the man's waist.

Davidson later threatened a lawsuit until he found out the man at the press gate was set up by Fred Haney, a good friend of Davidson's and mine.

The sixties saw the advent of the agent, to baseball's collective dismay, and I feel partly responsible. When Koufax and Drysdale were holding out, I said I would not negotiate with their agent, Bill Hayes. I said I would not negotiate with any agent, ever. Well, I broke that promise to myself once, and to this day I feel guilty about it.

Jimmy Lefebvre, the National League Rookie of the Year in 1965, brought in Larue Harcourt to see me one day. Larue was an assistant professor of some sort. Jimmy asked me if it would be all right to have Larue represent him, not in salary negotiations, but as an investment consultant. If that's what they wanted to do, I thought, that was fine with me.

Little did I know. Larue Harcourt later became a prominent agent, representing Don Sutton and Bob Forsch, among others.

The Dodgers were ahead of their time in another matter, too. In 1964, we instituted pay television, by which viewers could see our games on home television for a fee. Frank Sims, now the Angels' traveling secretary, was hired to do play-by-play, along with Fresco Thompson.

It didn't last long. Theater owners united and pay television was declared unconstitutional.

One of my final official acts with the Dodgers was overseeing the January and June drafts in 1968. It was a tribute to keen eyes and hard work. Al Campanis and Bill Schweppe, now vice presidents with the Dodgers, played significant roles.

The scouts did a remarkable job. It was the best group of players ever to come out of one draft, though at the time we had no idea it would be so strong.

In the January draft, we selected Davey Lopes in the second round and Geoff Zahn in the ninth round. In the regular phase of the June draft, we took Bobby Valentine first, Bill Buckner second, Joe Ferguson sixth, Tom Paciorek forticth, and Doyle Alexander forty-second. In the secondary phase, we took Steve Garvey first, Sandy Vance second, and Ron Cey third.

Our scouts were convinced Valentine would eventually be a star. Only a severely broken leg may have kept him from greatness. The scouts also figured Buckner would be a quality major-league hitter.

Otherwise, we weren't sure of anything. Although we drafted Garvey in the first round of the secondary phase, he was as much a sentimental choice as anything. His father, Joe, had been our bus driver for years in Florida, and as a kid Steve was always hanging around.

Cey's running ability was a concern to us. It wasn't so much how fast he ran, but the way he ran, which earned him the nickname "Penguin."

At the time, we had three categories for players.

The first consisted of fill-in players, those needed to
fill in minor-league rosters. The second was a money
category, players we thought we could sell for $7,500
or more. The third category included players we
were fairly certain had ability enough to play in the
major leagues.

Obviously, players drafted in the 40th and 42nd
rounds, like Paciorek and Alexander, were in the fill-
in category. Valentine and Buckner, on the other
hand, fell into category number three.

Fortunately, money was not an issue. Every one of
those boys was in it to play baseball. I doubt if the
entire draft cost us $200,000. By today's standards, it
was a steal.

Valentine was the most difficult player to sign. He
had had a sensational high school career, and he had
the Eastern press behind him. The New York newspapermen all sided with him.

Fresco Thompson called me from New York and
said he was having some trouble with Valentine, who
wanted $65,000 to sign. We had been offering him
$60,000. I told Fresco to give him the other $5,000.
For a player of that caliber, an extra $5,000 was
worth it.

Out of that draft came three-fourths of an infield
that would play together more years than any infield
in history: Garvey at first base, Lopes at second, and
Cey at third. Bill Russell, a selection in the 1966
draft, was the shortstop in that group.

The sixties provided me with many thrills. Koufax
pitched four no-hitters, Wills stole 104 bases in one
year, the Dodgers won pennants in '63, '65, and '66,
and in 1968 Drysdale established major league records for consecutive shutouts, six.

The last batter Drysdale faced in his sixth shutout
was the Giants' Dick Dietz, who came to the plate

with the bases loaded. Drysdale threw a pitch that was inches inside and Dietz did not move. He let the ball hit him, which would have allowed a run to score. Instead, the umpire disallowed the hit batsman, because Dietz had made no attempt to move out of the way of the pitch.

With two strikes on him, Dietz then popped the ball toward first baseman Wes Parker. I was at the game, and I jumped up and yelled as loud as I could, "If you drop that, Parker, you'll be in Spokane tomorrow!" It was a stupid thing to say, but the excitement of that great moment got the best of me.

It was the last bit of baseball history I was to witness as an employee of the Dodgers.

11

Lasorda:
A Pro and a Con

The cast of characters with whom I've been associated over the years is diverse, but no one character stands out as much as Tommy Lasorda, the clown prince of pasta.

Tommy has been good for the game. He's been as good for Tommy as he has been for the game, of course, but he has been an extraordinary ambassador of baseball.

He has never done anything to embarrass the game. Never. I find this remarkable, because he has certainly had the opportunity. He has a tendency to associate with all kinds of people.

I was amused by a March, 1986, issue of *Sports Illustrated*, which contained a special report on sports gambling. The article referred to Lasorda's association with Joe DeCarlo, a reputed associate of organized crime figures and assorted bookmakers. I'm not sure what the magazine was implying about Lasorda.

Tommy has never made a bet in his life. About 21 years ago, when Lasorda was scouting for the Dodgers, we went to see a high school game, where Jim Gilliam's son was playing center field. On the way, we stopped by Hollywood Park to bet a race or two. I gave Tommy $20 to make a couple of bets for himself.

As we were leaving the track for the game, I asked Tommy how he fared.

"What do you mean?" he asked.

"How much did you win or lose?"

"I didn't lose anything. I didn't make a bet. I've still got the twenty."

As Pete Rose said, when you go to lunch or dinner with DeCarlo, he'll pick up the tab. I'm sure that's the reason Tommy associates with DeCarlo.

Regardless, Tommy was never guilty of any wrong-doing. He is baseball's greatest public relations man. Of course, whatever he says about the game he says in a way that is designed to help his own image, too. That's OK, though, as long as he produces on the field. Peter O'Malley treats him the way I treated Drysdale and Koufax. They could do virtually anything they wanted, as long as they produced.

Walter O'Malley was fond of Lasorda. In fact, Walter was responsible for Lasorda's brief stay in the major leagues with the Dodgers, in 1954 and 1955. He pitched eight games and 13 innings for Brooklyn.

In 1954, Walter O'Malley had been to Montreal and he saw this pitcher who impressed him. His name was Tommy Lasorda, and Tommy had conned him, as he usually does everyone he meets. Consequently, Walter made a recommendation based more on personality than ability.

"We've got a left-handed pitcher at Montreal who looks pretty good," Walter said. Curious, I asked him which one.

"Tommy Lasorda," O'Malley said.

"Walter, he can't pitch here. He's a good boy, he's a good minor-league player. But he can't pitch in the major leagues."

"If you've got room for him, why don't you bring him up and give him a shot."

What could I say? O'Malley owned the club. It was probably the only time Walter ever asked me to do something regarding player personnel. So we brought Tommy up.

In the first inning of his first game, against St. Louis, Lasorda was forced to cover the plate after a throw home had gotten away from Campy. Wally Moon, then with the Cardinals, slid hard, and his spikes tore a gash in Lasorda's leg. Tommy needed stitches, it was obvious to everyone.

Walter Alston went to the mound where an argument ensued. Alston wanted to remove Tommy so he could get his leg sewn up. Tommy refused to come out. "It took me 10 years to get here," he told Walter, "and I'm not about to come out now."

In the spring of 1955, we had to make a roster decision. To round out the staff, we needed a left-handed pitcher. It was between Lasorda, 27, and a wild young lefty who was 19. We kept the youngster, to the chagrin of Lasorda, who could not understand why we'd keep this kid Koufax instead of him.

I called Lasorda into my office and offered him $800 a month to pitch for our Montreal farm club again. He had already pitched there five full seasons, and before he was through playing, he would spend another four seasons there.

"No," he said, declining the offer. Another year in Montreal did not appeal to him. "I'm quitting."

"Do you have a job lined up?" I asked.

"No."

"Do you want me to help you get a job?"

"Gee, that would be great, Buzzie, could you do that for me?"

I picked up the phone and called Al Moore, a former outfielder for the New York Giants, who then was the general manager of Rheingold Brewery.

"Al, can you use a young man over there? Tommy Lasorda?" I asked.

"I know Tommy, sure," Al said.

"He's retiring from baseball and he wants to get a job."

"Ask him if he can drive a truck."

"Tommy, can you drive a truck?"

"I can learn," Lasorda said.

"Yeah, he said he can learn to drive a truck."

"Tell him I'll give him $50 a week."

I told Tommy he had a job driving a truck at $50 a week and he was ecstatic.

"Gee, thanks, Buzzie. You're a great guy," he said. "I never thought you'd do that for me."

We shook hands and he walked out the door. I knew he'd be back. Seconds later, he returned.

"Wait a minute," Tommy said. "Fifty dollars a week, that's only $200 a month. And you offered me $800 a month to go to Montreal? I'll go to Montreal."

Lasorda's last game was a memorable one, although I remember it somewhat differently than Lasorda. It was in 1960, and he was still pitching at Montreal. I had offered him a job as a scout, and he had accepted it. This would be his last game.

I heard Tommy tell this version of his final hurrah on Rev. Robert Schuller's television program a few years ago.

It was at Rochester, and since it was his last game, he wanted more than ever to pitch well. In the first inning, he walked the first man. He hit the second batter in the back, then gave up an infield single to load the bases with nobody out.

"I looked over at the dugout and the manager is up on the steps," Lasorda told Schuller's audience. "I know if I don't get the next man I'm gone. So I turned around and looked up at the Big Dodger in the Sky and asked for help.

"Then I threw the ball as hard as I could to home plate and the man hit a vicious line drive. I never saw a ball hit so hard in my life. It went right to the third baseman, who threw to the second baseman, who threw to the first baseman, a triple play."

A few months later, I saw Lasorda. I said, "Tommy, I heard that story you told on Robert Schuller's program. It's a great story. You told it exactly as it was, except you added one word."

"What was that?"

"You said it was a triple play. Wasn't it a triple?"

What Tommy lacked in ability, he made up in determination. One spring, Tommy developed a plan to impress Dodger management: He was going to pitch to every batter in camp. We had 27 teams and about 600 players in camp back then. His idea was to start early in the morning and pitch to the Class D clubs first, then to the C clubs, until he had pitched his way through the entire system, including the Dodgers. He wanted to impress us with his durability.

Alston called me aside and said, "He can't do that. He'll kill himself."

"That's the trouble," I said, "he'll do it until he drops dead. Under no circumstances is he permitted to do it." I have no doubt that had we let him, he would have done it, or dropped dead trying.

Even when Lasorda was a youngster, he was not much different from what he is today. If there were five or fifty people in a room, you still knew he was there. Tommy has a reputation today for never paying for anything. Well, he never paid for anything then, either. There is one difference: today he can afford to pay for everything he gets for free.

When Tommy's daughter, Laura, was a little girl, she came to me one day and said, "Can't you make Daddy buy me the ice skates he promised me?"

"Ice skates? This is July," I said.

"Yeah, but he promised them to me in December," she said.

So I went to Tommy and asked him why he hadn't bought his little girl the ice skates.

"I'm waiting for a deal, Buzzie," Tommy said. "You know me. I'll get a deal somewhere."

Tommy was the sort who would go to New York with his wife Jo and walk down Broadway to Seventh Avenue, where all the dress manufacturers are, and he'd go into a place and say, "I'm here to see Mr. Schwartz."

"Which one, Solly or Ollie?" the girl would ask.

"Whichever one is in."

"Neither one is here right now."

"Darn," Tommy would say. "They told me to come in and pick out a suit for my wife."

Then, he'd be ushered upstairs and he'd get a suit for his wife, and Jo would ask later, "How do you know Mr. Schwartz?"

"I don't know any Schwartz," Lasorda would say. "You've got to figure there's a Schwartz in every dress place."

Tommy could always talk. It was and still is his greatest attribute. He was a good scout because of his ability to spin a yarn. He was especially good at selling a rookie's parents on the idea that signing with the Dodgers was in the best interest of their boy.

For instance, he did an excellent job signing Willie Crawford. Of course, it cost us $100,000, but Charlie Finley of the A's wanted Crawford, too. The Dodgers

got Crawford because of Tommy. He was a con artist.
That's what you needed in scouting then, before the
advent of the amateur draft.

Tommy and I went to scout the Dorsey Tournament
in Los Angeles one year, but we arrived late and saw
only the last inning of a game involving Los Angeles
High. This kid named Marshall was playing first
base. The first batter hit the ball to second base. The
next man flied to center field. The last man struck
out and the game was over.

Two months later, I was perusing the scouting
reports, and I came across a report on this boy
Marshall. I looked at it and it was signed by Tommy
Lasorda. The report said, "Has chance. Great arm.
Good power to right field. Above average runner.
Good hustler."

I called Tommy in and said, "Tommy, I was with
you that day. This kid never went to bat and he never
threw the ball. You got this from another scout, didn't
you?"

"Yeah," he said, laughing.

Lasorda and I went to San Diego once to see our
Spokane club play the old San Diego Padres of the
Pacific Coast League. I suggested we take a ride to
Tijuana, Mexico, for the afternoon.

Just after we crossed the border, we saw a grand-
stand and heard some noise, and there was a baseball
game in progress. It was pretty shoddy. No one had
uniforms and the field was a mess. But the kids were
playing like hell.

We noticed this kid playing center field. He could
go and get the ball as well as anyone we'd seen. He
made one catch over his head that was reminiscent of
the famous catch Willie Mays made on Vic Wertz. At
the plate, the kid doubled and tripled.

"Tommy, let's grab this kid," I said. We had it all

planned out. We'd bring him to the United States and put him in school, and when he graduated from high school, we'd sign him.

Tommy, who speaks fluent Spanish, went over to talk with the manager about this kid. Suddenly, I heard this roar. Everyone was laughing. When Tommy returned, I asked him what happened.

"I'll tell you later," he said. "Let's get out of here."

We got in the car and I asked him again what had happened and why everyone was laughing.

"I was talking to the manager about this fellow," Tommy said, "and he said, 'Yeah, he's a good player. But we can only use him three hours a day.' I asked him why. 'Because he has to go back to the nuthouse,' the manager told me. They get him out of the insane asylum once a week just to play the game. Then they have to return him."

I was as surprised as anyone that Lasorda eventually became the manager of the Dodgers. I never thought that would happen. It never entered my mind, because Tommy was hard to take seriously. Number one, he was a practical joker. Number two, he had limited ability. He never impressed anyone with his knowledge of the game. But he did have a great personality.

Perhaps the only reason he became a coach under Alston in 1973 was the long-standing Dodger policy of promoting loyal employees to allow them to qualify for the pension.

In all my years with the Dodgers, we always brought up a minor-league manager or a scout or even retired players to be coaches, to get them their required years. We did it with Joe Becker. We did it with Pete Reiser and Lefty Phillips. We even brought Sandy Amoros back for 30 days to make sure he qualified for the pension.

Tommy would be the first to admit it, I'm sure. Walter Alston would not have chosen Tommy as one of his coaches. It probably was done as a favor to Tommy, by the Dodger brass.

Today, Lasorda is a commodity in great demand. With his personality alone, Tommy is putting customers in the seats. The competition for the entertainment dollar is so great these days, something more is necessary than merely opening the gates. This is where Tommy is so effective.

Sparky Anderson has a little bit of Lasorda in him. The clubs that have colorful managers always seem to do well at the gate. New York with Casey Stengel always did well. As bad as he behaved off the field, Billy Martin still put people in the seats because (a) he could manage, and (b) his volatile personality and off-the-field actions caught the public's attention.

Lasorda is many things. He is part comedian, part con. He is an exceptional storyteller and an entertainer in his own right. He is a career baseball man, although baseball really isn't his forte. Talking about it is.

If he is baseball's best showman, he is, too, its greatest salesman.

12

The Son Also Rises: Leaving LA

By 1968, I could see the son rising, and in the process, the sun setting on my Dodger career. The son was Peter O'Malley, whose father, Walter, had been grooming him for my job, and rightfully so. I was aware that blood is thicker than water, but it did not make leaving my life behind any easier.

The Dodgers were my life. I had worked for the club since 1938, 30 years of fun and games, but the time had come to move on. Leaving was difficult. I knew I would miss the O'Malleys. They were wonderful people. So were those with whom I worked, notably Fresco Thompson, Al Campanis, Bill Schweppe, Red Patterson, and Billy DeLury.

At least I wasn't going far, and it was in every regard an upward move. I was to become a part-owner of a National League expansion franchise, the San Diego Padres. If I had left to go to an established club, I'd have felt bad, as if I had betrayed the

O'Malleys. In my mind, I justified it by the fact I
would be building a new club.

I knew eventually I would have to leave the Dodger
organization to make room for Peter O'Malley. That
day was growing closer, so the San Diego opportunity
came at a propitious time. Again, Walter had used
the phrase, "You've got to get something that will
stick to your ribs." He was completely supportive of
my move to San Diego.

The idea to lure me away from the Dodgers was
that of C. Arnholt Smith, a prominent banker who
had owned the minor-league version of the San Diego
Padres for a number of years. He had long been
unsuccessful in bringing a major league club to San
Diego, but it was suggested to him that I possessed
the contacts necessary to pull it off.

Smith then called O'Malley to ask permission to
talk with me, to see if I'd be interested in running an
expansion franchise in San Diego and owning a part
of the club.

Originally, it appeared a club would play in Seattle, an idea Walter had been pushing. In the mean-
time, I received a call from Smith. He said if I could
get the franchise for him, he'd give me 32 percent of
the club as my fee. That was a lucrative offer.

I told Walter about the offer I had from Smith. At
first, Walter was opposed to the idea. He confused C.
Arnholt with his brother, who was called Black Jack
Smith. In retrospect, it is too bad Walter wasn't
opposed to C. Arnholt; I'd have been better off as a
result.

The cities under consideration for expansion franchises were Montreal, Denver, Dallas, Buffalo, and
San Diego. And at the league meeting in July, Montreal and San Diego were the winners. The time had
come for me to leave the Dodgers.

I still had some business to take care of with the

Dodgers, so I did not resign immediately. However, Walter wanted me out immediately—to get me off the payroll, I guess.

Walter said to me, "Bob Carpenter [of the Phillies] thinks it's a conflict of interest that you're still here."

"You've got to be kidding," I said. "We don't even have one ballplayer in San Diego yet. How can it be a conflict of interest?"

I wrote a letter to John Quinn, the general manager of the Phillies, and he answered, "What the hell are you talking about? Carpenter doesn't know anything about this. He doesn't care whether you stay there all year."

Walter apparently cared, though. So I decided to leave on a Monday.

"No, you've got to stay until Wednesday," Walter said. "The players want to do something for you."

"Oh, yeah? What?"

He couldn't wait to tell me. "They're going to give you a motorboat."

"Well, this puts me in good company," I said. "The Brooklyn Dodger players gave Mr. Rickey a motorboat when he left the Dodgers."

"Yeah," he said, maintaining his disregard for Mr. Rickey until the end, "but the players got *that* one wholesale."

Prior to the expansion draft in October, I received a call from O'Malley, who needed help in determining which 40 players in the organization he should protect. It was Fresco Thompson's job, but Fresco had been hospitalized. I agreed to help Walter.

On the way to Dodger Stadium, Evit and I stopped at St. Jude's Hospital in Fullerton to visit Fresco. His wife, Peg, was in the lobby, in tears. She had just been told that Fresco was in real bad shape.

I went up to see Fresco, and told him I was doing

his job for him, that I was going to Los Angeles to
help Walter.

"That's fine, Buzzie," Fresco said, "but who are you
going to take in the draft?"

"Bill Russell, Jeff Torborg, and Jim Brewer," I
said, mentioning three players the Dodgers were not
planning on protecting.

"Oh, you can't do that, particularly Russell and
Brewer. Russell's a fine prospect."

"That's why I'm taking him," I said.

"You can't do that," Fresco pleaded. "Buzzie, don't
do that to me, really."

"Who do you want me to take?"

"Why don't you take somebody like Al Ferrara and
Jim Williams?"

He told me the three players to take. "OK, I'll do it
for you," I said, knowing I was going to be crucified
in the press. Dick Young, then of the *New York Daily
News*, was the only writer who knew why I did what
I did. I had spoken with the doctor, who had told me
that Fresco was dying and that he wasn't going to
make it. I knew I had to keep my promise.

I went to Dodger Stadium and met with Walter
O'Malley and Walter Alston. I said, "You can't leave
Brewer on the unprotected list. If you leave him there
and I don't draft him, people are going to crucify
me."

Brewer had had 14 saves in 1968. I talked them
into including Brewer on the protected list, which
took the heat off me. Leaving Russell unprotected
was OK, because nobody knew him at the time.

We did not draft Russell, who went on to play in
more games than any Los Angeles Dodger in history.
The three players we settled on were Ferrara, Williams, and Zoilo Versalles.

As I was about to leave the meeting with the two

Walters, O'Malley said to me, "You know what's happened since you left here, Buzzie? We've lost $2 million."

"No kidding, Walter," I said, and I smiled.

Walking out, Alston said to me, "Damn, Buzzie, you're great."

"What do you mean?"

"You know Walter. When he loses money, he gets mad and people are going to get fired. He lost $2 million. You know that, and yet you laughed."

"Walter," I said, laughing again, "what he meant is that he didn't make $6 million this year, he only made $4 million.

We were doomed from the beginning in San Diego under the ownership of C. Arnholt Smith. He was the owner of the United States National Bank, which became the largest bank failure in the nation's history to that point.

When he got the franchise, his financial empire had already begun to crumble. I had anticipated we'd get into the league for $7 million. When I learned the price would be $10 million, I advised Smith to back out. At that price, we would not have enough money left to properly operate the club. He went ahead and got the franchise anyway.

He never understood baseball or anything necessary to run a club. He would not allow us to spend money, failing to understand that you had to sign players for the four minor-league clubs.

By the time he was forced to sell, money was so scarce we could not afford to sign anyone. We had a chance to sign Doug DeCinces, but Smith could afford to offer him only a $4,000 bonus. Doug wanted enough to guarantee his college education, or about $6,000. The Padres did not sign DeCinces because they could not afford the extra $2,000. I suppose we could have taken up a collection and put up our own money, but no one was about to do that.

Every time we got a decent player, we would have to sell him. It had come to the point where we'd pay the players on a Friday and ask them not to cash their checks until Monday.

Early in the 1970 season, the Giants and Willie Mays arrived for a weekend series in San Diego. Giants manager Clyde King, a long-time friend, informed me that Mays, who had 599 home runs at the time, would be rested in the series opener Friday night.

That gave us an idea for a promotion. In the past, our attendance had always been so low we never had reason to open the bleachers in left field. So we announced at the game Friday night that on Saturday, for the first time, we were going to open the bleachers in left field, and that anyone lucky enough to catch Willie Mays's 600th career home run would win a new Chevrolet. We got the Chevrolet people to donate the car.

We put the tickets on sale at the game Friday night and sold about 1,200 of them at $3 a head. That represented a pretty good payday for us. Remember, money was scarce in those days.

So with two outs in the ninth inning of Friday night's game, who do you think Clyde King sent in to pinch hit? Up to the plate came Willie Mays. He hit a home run into the vacant bleachers in left field.

We had to refund the money.

In 1974, when we were still watching every dollar, we were robbed again. Lou Brock and the St. Louis Cardinals came to town, when Brock had 103 stolen bases, one shy of Maury Wills's major league record. In the third inning, he stole second to tie Wills. The 4,000 people there gave him a standing ovation, when suddenly, the umpire went over to second base, picked up the bag, and gave it to Brock. That base cost $52. I was seething, though there was nothing I could do about it.

In the seventh inning, Brock singled and promptly stole second base, his 105th stolen base of the year and a new record. And the damn umpire gave him another base. We lost $104 worth of bases that day.

C. Arnholt Smith was not only broke, he was ignorant about baseball matters. This was particularly apparent when he was forced to sell the club. In 1973, he was in Washington, D.C., and Joe Danzansky, a grocery store magnate who wanted to move the club to the nation's capital, offered Smith $12.5 million for the Padres. Smith immediately accepted the offer, failing to realize that (a) he needed permission from the league to sell the club and (b) he had to get out of the stadium lease with the city of San Diego.

Smith had to sell the club in the first place because he was in trouble with the law over income tax evasion and grand theft. He was accused of stealing millions of dollars from firms he controlled. These were his own problems, but because I was part-owner of the Padres, they became my problems, too.

The club had nothing to do with the allegations against Smith, though the government did not realize this. Therefore, I was called to testify in court.

"Isn't it true," the district attorney asked me on the stand, "that in the five years Mr. Smith owned the Padres that he took $7.5 million out of the ball club?"

I laughed, and the DA said, "This is not a laughing matter."

I turned to the judge and said, "Your honor, he'd have to be a magician to take $7.5 million out of the club, because we didn't do that much business in five years."

Investors in the U.S. National Bank were eventually awarded civil fraud damages totaling $30 million against Smith. An IRS agent came to my office and told me Smith owed $26,753,420.42 in back taxes for one year. I reached into my pocket and took out 42 cents and said, "Here, how about my making it even?" He didn't think that was funny.

When Smith was convicted, the government took my 32 percent of the club to help pay his back taxes, which in my opinion they had no right to do. In retrospect, that was fine with me. If he was in trouble, the least I could do was help him. After all, he had given me the opportunity to become an owner. In the aftermath, two attorneys tried to persuade me to take the matter to court, but I wouldn't do it. I came to San Diego with nothing, so I lost nothing.

We would eventually sell the club for $12.5 million. But we owed Chemical Bank in New York about $3 million, which was a demand note to the club, and by our arrangement with the league, Chemical Bank was to be paid off first. That left $9.5 million. We used $300,000 to pay local debts and $1.2 million to pay off debts to the city. That left about $8 million, of which I was entitled to 32 percent, or $2.56 million. There was no reason for Uncle Sam to confiscate my $2.56 million, but he did. I never received a dime from the sale of the club.

Smith, meanwhile, had been granted approval by the National League to sell the club to Danzansky, with the understanding that the city of San Diego would give the club a release from its stadium contract.

Smith assumed that the release would not be a problem, and he proceeded to prepare the club for its transfer. We had everything packed and ready to move. The new manager had already been selected, too. Danzansky's choice was Minnie Minoso.

I wasn't going with the club, however. I had decided I did not want to leave. I was going to retire and do something else.

Then the sale fell through. John Witt, the city attorney for San Diego, filed a suit against the National League and its members, seeking damages for breaking the lease at San Diego Stadium. When Danzansky would not indemnify the league against losses in the suit, the sale was off. The Padres were still in San Diego and I was back in business.

13

Hold the Tomato: Life with Ray Kroc

Ray Kroc must have turned over in his grave the day McDonald's came out with its new hamburger, the McD.L.T. Ray detested tomatoes. He did not think they belonged on hamburgers, and while he was still alive, McDonald's did not serve tomatoes on its burgers.

Kroc was the McDonald's hamburger magnate, the man responsible for putting the gold in McDonald's arches. By the time the count on the number of McDonald's burgers served reached a billion, Ray was wealthy enough that he could afford to buy any toy he wished. He chose to buy the Padres.

He was the third person to make an offer on the club. The first was Joseph Danzansky, who wanted to move the club to Washington, D.C. The second was Marje Everett, the owner of Hollywood Park race track. Marje, whose group included songwriter Burt Bacharach, was going to buy the club and leave it in

San Diego. She made an offer equal to the amount Danzansky had offered, $12.5 million.

On the assumption she would own the team, she proposed a transaction that would turn things around in San Diego. She decided that what we needed in San Diego was a player with an established name. "Why don't you try to get somebody like McCovey?" her attorney, Neil Papiano, said to me, based on Marje's suggestion.

That was fine with me, as long as she wanted to pay the salary. Based entirely on the fact that she would soon be the owner, we acquired McCovey. And Marje was right. The season before we had McCovey, we drew about 550,000. The first season we had him, we drew more than one million. McCovey was responsible.

McCovey was Big Mac, after whom the hamburger was NOT named, and manager John McNamara was Little Mac. We certainly took advantage of Big Mac. One day, McCovey paid visits to several of the McDonald's franchises in the area and sold $30,000 worth of tickets for us.

But Marje Everett's bid to buy the club had failed, and it appeared the National League would have to assume control of the club until a buyer could be found. Then I received a call from Don Lubin, a lawyer in Chicago.

"I understand the club is for sale," he said. "I have a client who'd like to purchase the club."

"Who is it?" I asked. "What's the group?"

"Ray Kroc."

"Oh," I said, unimpressed.

"Well, he happens to have 7.5 million shares of McDonald's stock."

I did not know who Ray Kroc was at the time, but we made a date for him to come to San Diego to discuss the sale. I called my son Peter who was working for the club, too, and explained the offer to him. I said I didn't think this Ray Kroc realized the cost of the club was $12.5 million.

I had never been to a McDonald's hamburger stand. When he said McDonald's stock, I thought maybe he meant McDonnell stock, as in McDonnell Douglas, the airplane company, whose stock was selling for about $2.50 a share at the time. "How can he afford $12.5 million?" I asked.

Peter left the room and came back a few minutes later and said, "Dad, you've got the wrong McDonald's. He has stock in the fast-food chain and that's selling for about $45 a share."

Seven-and-a-half million shares of McDonald's stock at $45 a share was $337.5 million. Ray Kroc could afford to buy the Padres, or anything else, for that matter.

Kroc and his representatives arrived, and he and Smith agreed on the sale for $12,250,000. Then Smith balked.

"Wait a minute," he said. "I didn't realize that you were buying the assets, which means the bank accounts, too."

The man was a banker; he knew the meaning of the word *asset*.

"We can't do it," Smith said. "We'll have to have more money if you're going to take over the bank accounts, too."

"How much more?" Ray's attorney asked.

"Five hundred thousand dollars more," Smith said.

We had $1,200 in the bank. Nothing more. Ray knew it, but he didn't want to haggle. He agreed to give him an extra $250,000. When you have nearly $350 million, what is $250,000?

After the deal had been consummated, Ray Kroc's picture suddenly began appearing on magazine covers, and to his amusement he became a media figure.

"If I'd spent $12 million for an office building," he said, "no one would have cared."

Ray was a savior of sorts in San Diego; the people fell in love with him from day one. He was introduced before the Padres' home opener in his first season, 1974, and received a standing ovation.

Midway through the game, he became a hero as well. The Padres had a runner on first, and the batter hit a foul pop-up to the first baseman. The runner on first was inexcusably caught off base for a double play.

Ray, who enjoyed a drink from time to time and undoubtedly had had a few on this night, went to the public address announcer's booth and took over the microphone. At precisely that moment, a streaker ran across the field and Ray yelled out—into the microphone, unfortunately—"Arrest that SOB!"

Without ever identifying himself, Ray then began addressing the crowd, and the crowd knew immediately who was speaking.

"That was the most stupid baseball I've ever seen in my life," Kroc said in part. He apologized to the fans and promised that things would get better. He was chastised by the media and the players for his actions, but as a public relations move it was nothing short of a stroke of genius. The fans loved it.

I had only heard part of what he had said, as I'd been investigating a leak in the equipment room downstairs. On my way back up, I heard him thanking the fans for their attendance, that we had outdrawn the Dodgers in their home opener.

"Gee, that's a nice thing for the owner of a club to do," I thought to myself. That was the first time that had ever been done, I was sure.

I went back upstairs, where I was met by the reporters. They asked me what I thought of Ray's performance.

"I thought it was fine. It's the first time an owner of a club has thanked the public over the public address system."

"What about the rest of it?"

"What rest of it?"

They told me what he had said, but what could I do about it? It was too late.

Later that season, Ray held a party at his massive condominium on Michigan Avenue in Chicago. George Halas, then the owner of the Chicago Bears and a friend of Ray's, was there.

"Damn, Ray," Halas said to him, "I've wanted to do something like that for 40 years, but I never had the guts."

Charlie O. Finley, the owner of the Oakland A's at the time and a Chicago resident, was at the same party and he agreed wholeheartedly.

On Ray's first day as owner of the Padres, he went down to the offices and immediately gave everyone a raise. He did not fire anyone, either. He was a very generous man.

Before the season opener in 1976, he threw a little party at the Westgate Hotel, where he stood up and said he had an announcement to make. He said he had just set up an irrevocable trust, leaving 60 percent of the club to his wife, Joan, five percent to my son, Peter, five percent to his son-in-law, Ballard Smith, 15 percent to McDonald's chairman of the board Fred Miller, and 15 percent to his good friend Buzzie.

Good gravy, I thought, no one had ever done anything like that for us before. Actually, it became a moot point for the Bavasis, because when Peter left to start up the Toronto Blue Jays, he told Ray's lawyer he couldn't accept part ownership of another club. When I left to go to the Angels, I called the lawyer and told him that I couldn't accept it, either. Although it was an irrevocable trust, it would represent a conflict of interest.

It was a nice gesture, anyway. Ray came into my office after I had resigned in 1978 and said, "Buzzie, you and I have had a good time. I'm going to pay you your whole salary for the rest of the year and 50 percent of your salary for next year."

"Ray," I said, "if I'd known you were going to be that generous, I would have retired two years ago."

He did give me a financial tip that I failed to act on. He told me to take the money and put it into McDonald's stock and Disney stock. Disney went up to $120 a share and McDonald's is up to about $80 a share now.

Ray was as lucky as he was smart, and in one instance, he may have been both. One season, we had a promotion whereby every time we won a Sunday home game, each fan in attendance would get a free hamburger from McDonald's merely by showing a ticket stub.

Luck was a factor, because we played about 10 Sunday home games that year and we won once. On the other hand, Ray may have been smart. The odds were against our winning *any* game.

When we finally won a Sunday home game, it caused a massive problem. After the game, everyone went to the closest McDonald's, near the ballpark. That franchise almost went out of business.

Ray was a man of impulse. He'd act on the emotion of the moment, though never with malicious intent. On the first day of his first regular season as owner, the Padres were playing in San Francisco.

Since we had acquired McCovey to play first, we had to move Nate Colbert to left field. In the first inning, Colbert allowed a ball to bounce over his head for a triple, scoring two runs.

"Get rid of that son of a bitch!" Ray screamed. "Get

rid of him right now! I don't want him around
tomorrow!"

"Yessir," I said.

In the seventh inning, Colbert hit one about a mile
that put us out in front, 3–2. This time, Ray was on his
feet, clapping and cheering.

"Sit down, Ray," I whispered to him. "Sit down."

"Why should I sit down?" he said. "Did you see
that?"

"Yes, Ray, but we got rid of him in the first inning."

One Saturday evening, he called me up at 6 o'clock
and asked me to go to Atlanta to fire our manager,
John McNamara. I arrived at the park on Sunday and
was having lunch with Phil Collier, a respected
baseball writer for the *San Diego Union*, and John
Mattei, our traveling secretary, who wondered why I
was there.

"Do you know how to say a Hail Mary?" I said. "Say
one for John."

We were playing a doubleheader with the Braves,
and we won the first game. Then we won the second
game. I never did see John. I went back to the airport
and called Ray. He had been listening to the games on
the radio, of course, and he was ecstatic about winning a doubleheader. He never did mention John's
name to me.

Ray was a delightful man to be around, except
when he was driving. You never wanted to be in an
automobile with him, unless he had a chauffeur
driving. I thought I was the world's worst driver
until I met Ray. If I put a dent in my car, a Toyota or
a Chevy, it didn't matter much. But his cars were
always Cadillacs, Rolls Royces, or Excalibers. A
fender dent in one of those cars cost as much to fix as
my car cost to buy.

He came to spring training in Yuma one day in a
chauffeur-driven white Rolls Royce, and decided to

visit the local McDonald's. Ray liked to go into Mc-
Donald's franchises when he was not expected. A
fanatic for cleanliness, he would inspect the grounds
on the outside first. The outside of this Yuma McDonald's was spotless. He went inside and everything was
spotless there, also. He talked to the manager for a
few minutes and we left.

On the way back to the camp, he said, "You know,
I think he [the McDonald's manager] knew I was
coming. Somebody must have tipped him off."

"Of course not," I said. "In Yuma? Every day, 10 or
15 chauffeur-driven white Rolls Royces come into
McDonald's. He wouldn't know it was you."

In San Diego, Ray would periodically come into my
office and ask me to go to a McDonald's with him.
We'd go to several different ones, and if they weren't
clean, he'd have a fit. I've seen him chew out two
managers in front of customers over something as
trivial as a napkin or a rag on the floor.

His impulsiveness carried over into his buying
habits. He wanted a home in La Jolla, so he employed
an agent I knew to take him around. He found a house
he liked and, without even inquiring about the price,
offered $1 million for it. The sellers accepted.

Later that day, Ray and Joan were discussing the
house and what they might do to the dining room.
They decided they needed to see the room again.

The following day they returned to the home and
knocked on the door. The maid answered. They
introduced themselves as the people who were buy-·
ing the house, and he asked if they could come in to
look at the dining room.

The maid said the owner of the house was indis-
posed, and asked that they come back later.

"No, I want to do it now," Ray said.

"You can't come in now," she said.

That was all Ray had to hear. He walked out and

went down the street and bought another house in five minutes. The people selling the first house probably lost a few hundred thousand dollars by not allowing Ray to inspect the dining room.

Ray knew how to live, I'll say that for him, and how to enjoy his money. Once when we were in Florida, he took us out to his house in Fort Lauderdale, and resting across the road was his 65-foot yacht. He also had a jet that could take him from San Diego to New York in about four hours.

By the same token, he would not give money away unless he felt it was earned. He loved to help children's hospitals. He contributed heavily to one in Chicago, and he was a staunch supporter of Danny Thomas's hospital in Memphis, Tennessee. But he would not donate to educational institutions or religious institutions. He felt that if people wanted an education, they should be willing to work for it.

Ray could be tough. We were having dinner one night in Chicago at a restaurant he visited frequently. The dinner was excellent and the bill came to about $300. But Ray was not pleased with the service. When he paid the bill, he did not leave a tip. I could not understand why, but I did not want to start an argument.

"I don't leave tips unless I get the service I want," he said. "That's what I pay for. This was terrible service and the owner knows it was terrible service."

As we were leaving, I happened to see the owner, and I gave him $50 and told him to give it to the waiter.

"No, Mr. Bavasi," he said, "we can't do that. If Ray found out, he'd never come back."

In all the years I had been associated with the Dodgers, the club always had an in-house attorney. But the Padres didn't. I suggested that since Ray's

daughter Linda was married to attorney Ballard
Smith (who was the district attorney of Allegheny
County in Pennsylvania), that we should bring him in
as the club's vice president for the purpose of having
an in-house lawyer.

Then and there, Ballard Smith was hired. One of
his first assignments was to take over the local
hockey team, the San Diego Mariners of the Western
Hockey League. Like the Padres, the Mariners were
in pitiful shape. At the end of Ray's first year in San
Diego, the Mariners were on the verge of folding.

As a civic duty, the mayor of San Diego came to us
to see if we would help. Ray said he would take over
the club and its considerable debts, but that he would
not pay anything for the club itself.

I became president of the Mariners and Ballard
Smith became the general manager. He did an effective job, too, initiating several promotions to boost
attendance. One of his better promotions was booking
the Russian national hockey team to play an exhibition game with the Mariners. As it turned out, it was
not a diplomatic success.

At the time, the San Diego Chicken was in his first
year, and he was not yet self-employed. He was
working for a local radio station which had the call
letters KGB. He was known as the KGB Chicken, and
on the front of his chicken uniform were the station's
call letters.

The Chicken was working the hockey game that
night. He came bouncing down the steps, to the
delight of the crowd. Then the Russian hockey players saw him. And suddenly, all hell broke loose. The
Russians refused to play. I thought we were going to
have another war.

I could not find Ballard, who was in the locker
room with the coach. And we couldn't find anyone
who could speak Russian. Finally, we found the

team's interpreter, and I asked him what was the problem.

"They think you're making fun of their distinguished organization, the KGB," the interpreter said.

To no avail, I tried to explain to him that KGB was a local radio station and the Chicken was a mascot of sorts. He would not believe me until I showed him a press guide with all the local radio stations listed, including KGB.

Ray Kroc was a great baseball fan and an excellent businessman. Put them together, though, and he was lost. He did not understand the baseball business. In 1976, Ray made a statement that we had lost a lot of money. What we had done was *spend* a lot of money. That was the year we signed Rollie Fingers, George Hendrick, and Gene Tenace. Ray could not understand that to sign players, you had to spend money. You can't sign the players and keep your money, too.

The way I looked at it was that if you pay $700,000 for Rollie Fingers, that's the same as having $700,000 in the bank. But Ray could not see it that way.

George Hendrick has a tarnished reputation that he does not deserve. He is one of the finest young men I have ever met, and on every club for which he played, he was one of the most popular players among his teammates.

The media has portrayed him as a despicable character because he refuses to talk with the press. To an extent, I can understand why. When he played in Cleveland, a writer there wrote an unflattering story about him, and he took exception to it. He claimed the story contained several inaccuracies and misquotes. To prevent a repeat, he simply chose not to grant interviews.

It doesn't make him a bad person, does it? To the contrary, I found him delightful. When he played for the Padres, he would come into the office every day to talk baseball. "This isn't the man I've heard about," I thought to myself.

He was in the office one Saturday, and I said, "Don't forget, tomorrow is autograph day and you're scheduled to sign autographs from 12 to 12:30."

"Buzzie, you know I don't do those things," he said.

"What?" I asked, amazed.

"Every club I've been with, they know I don't do those things."

"Is that right, George? You're not going to be there tomorrow? OK. Would you do me a favor, then? Would you tell John McNamara that if you're not there tomorrow that the entire club will work out Monday morning [an off day] at 8:30, stop at noon for lunch, then work out until 4? Or better yet, you might tell the player rep."

George went downstairs and thought about it for a few minutes, and called back, as I was sure he would.

"Buzzie, do you mean it, that if I don't show up tomorrow for the autograph session you're going to make all 25 players work out Monday?"

"Yes."

"I'll be there," he said. He understood. He knew what might happen if 24 other players had to work out because he refused to show up for an autograph session.

Dave Winfield was a lot like Hendrick in one regard. He liked to come into the office and sit and talk baseball, which few players do anymore. Winfield was like Hendrick in another regard, too: he could swing a bat.

I loved to watch Winfield hit, though he could have become a pitcher with the Padres. When we signed him, we let him decide whether he wanted to pitch or be an everyday player.

Winfield was an exceptional athlete. He was

drafted by the Minnesota Vikings, though he'd never played college football. He was drafted by an NBA club, as well, and he was a superb basketball player for the Golden Gophers at the University of Minnesota.

He wanted a $125,000 bonus from us, which was out of the question at the time. This was 1973, before Ray Kroc owned the club. We convinced him to take $75,000, and today he earns $2 million a year. He never would have made that much playing football or basketball.

He had an 8–1 record as a pitcher in his senior year at Minnesota, and we were willing to let him pitch, if that had been his desire. He went home and thought about it for a day, then came back and said he preferred to play every day.

Winfield never played in the minor leagues; there wasn't much sense in sending him out. Our club was so bad that anybody could have played for us. We needed him. He was one of those players who did not need the benefit of spring training. He made an impact immediately. And by the time I left San Diego, he had earned his way onto my all-time team of players I employed.

John McNamara was fired as the Padres manager 48 games into the 1977 season, and he was replaced by Alvin Dark. Shortly thereafter, I decided to retire and I resigned as president of the Padres. My retirement was short-lived, though. Soon, I would be back in the saddle again, courtesy of Gene Autry.

One more example of how the game has changed: When I left San Diego, George Hendrick called to ask if I needed money. And to think I used to lend money to players.

14

Riding Shotgun
with the Cowboy:
The Angel Years

A winner all his life, Gene Autry had lost patience with losing. It wasn't so much the losses between the lines, but those on the bottom line. And the bottom line in any business is fiscal.

When Autry called, he was seeking someone to transform the California Angels from a money loser to a money maker. The man had not accrued his fortune by throwing it away, and he was intent on turning the franchise around.

I had no intention of working again. The thought of retirement appealed to me. I had received letters from friends in baseball, notably Bing Devine, Lee MacPhail, and Jim Campbell, all wishing me well. I had spent almost 40 years in the game at that point.

In my mind, I had retired. Evit and I wanted to travel, to see parts of America where professional baseball does not exist.

Then I received a call from Don Drysdale, who was

working as a broadcaster for the Angels. He said
Gene wanted to see me.

"They need someone to turn the thing around,"
Drysdale said. "They're losing a fortune."

"Gee, I don't think I want to go back to work," I
said, though I was flattered that someone was
interested.

"Well, do me a favor," Don said. "Just go over and
see Gene. I'll have him call you."

A meeting was scheduled in Palm Springs, where
Mr. Autry maintains a hotel and a home. I had known
Gene for 20 years, so we weren't strangers. We talked
for about an hour, and he made some suggestions that
made sense.

I told him I wasn't really interested in getting back
into the baseball business, but he persevered. He
asked that I come in for a few months to see what
could be done to save money as well as boost attendance to make money.

I asked him for some time to think about it, and we
set a date to meet after the 1977 season. At the
meeting, I agreed to come in—for one year only.

From the outset of my career with Gene, I knew
things were going to be a little difficult. To begin
with, the club was giving away too many complimentary tickets. We fixed that. Employees were still
entitled to tickets for themselves and their families,
but complimentary tickets for friends were disallowed. We reduced the number of free tickets we
issued from about 2,200 a game to 1,100 a game. The
only thing in baseball we have to sell is the ticket. If
you're going to give them away, why open the doors?

Every departmental assistant, it seemed, had an
assistant. And the club had too many trade-out accounts, for automobiles and restaurants. Mr. Autry
did not dine at those restaurants and he did not need
the automobiles, so who was benefitting?

We did not fire any employees, but we did not hire
additional help, either. What we did was give everyone an additional job, which seemed to work. At the
end of the 1977 season, the club was in debt for about
$3.5 million. By the end of the 1982 season, we had
paid that off and had put a substantial amount of
money in the bank, thanks to the efforts of Red
Patterson, who had had more time to devote to
promotional activities and his talent for filling up
empty seats.

What we had done was cut out wasteful spending
and put the money to use where it was needed. For
this, I received a reputation for being cheap. However, I myself fueled this reputation. I urged Jim
Healy, the controversial and popular radio sports
personality in Los Angeles, to call me "El Cheapo,"
the same phrase used to describe Branch Rickey in
Brooklyn.

On the air, Healy repeatedly called me El Cheapo,
which helped me save money. If people think you're
cheap, they don't expect too much. They don't come
bothering you for favors.

Harry Dalton, one of the bright young general
managers in the game, was handling player personnel when I joined the Angels, but I admit he was
probably looking over his shoulder when I was
brought to Anaheim. He understood he could make
any deal he deemed necessary, unless money was
involved. On matters involving money, he could do
nothing without my authority.

Undoubtedly, it cramped his style and he was
uncomfortable. When Harry received an attractive
offer from the Milwaukee Brewers, he had to take it.
And when he left, the Angels were without anyone to
oversee the baseball operation. So Gene asked if I'd
stay on for a while. I agreed. Once again, I was
operating a baseball club.

One of the saddest experiences of my life occurred during my second season with the Angels. Lyman Bostock, signed as a free agent in November of 1977, was shot and killed in Gary, Indiana on September 23, 1978.

I was in bed in La Jolla when I got a call about 8 A.M. on a Saturday morning to inform me that Bostock had been shot. There were no details. I was stunned. Later that day, I learned that Lyman had passed away.

The first thing I did was phone his wife to find out if the club could be of any help, and to let her know that Lyman's contract would, of course, be recognized and paid in full.

It was an incredible shock. Bostock had come to the Angels after three great years in Minnesota where he hit .282, .323, and .336 in consecutive seasons. You can only wonder what kind of career he might have had if his life hadn't been cut short so senselessly.

The bitter irony of Bostock's death was that I had insured his contract. I had never insured a player's contract before, basically because it wasn't necessary. The salaries hadn't been so exorbitant that the club had to be protected. Nor had there been any long-term contracts. Why I decided to take out insurance on Bostock's contract, I don't know.

Let me tell you how smart his agent was. I told him that Bostock should take out the insurance himself.

"How much will it cost?" the agent asked.

"Eleven thousand dollars," I said. "And you should do it instead of the club."

"Why should *we* do it?" he said.

"Because should something happen to Lyman, his estate or wife would be the beneficiary."

"But the contract's guaranteed. You'd have to pay him anyway."

"Fine," I said. "But let me explain it to you and you

can do what you want. If Lyman takes out the insurance himself and makes his wife the beneficiary and something happens to Lyman, she gets the money tax free. If we take it out, and we pay the guaranteed salary, it's ordinary income. She has to pay tax on it."

"Well, we're not going to do it."

"Lyman," I said later, "please get someone else to represent you."

When the tragedy occurred, Lyman still had about $1.8 million due him from the contract. His wife probably ended up with about half of that due to income taxes which could have been avoided had Lyman's agent had better sense.

The Bostock tragedy was a shock to everyone in the organization. He was a man of impeccable character. When he started slowly for the Angels in 1978, he came into my office and volunteered to give his first month's salary to charity. He did not feel he had earned it.

I would not let him do it. Charity begins at home, I said.

"You worked for it. If you had hit .900, I wouldn't give you any more money."

That he even made the offer spoke well of him. He was a fine young man. Of course, the good Lord doesn't take the bad ones. He only wants the good ones. They've got a heckuva club up there, I'll tell you that.

Between the 1978 and 1979 seasons, we traded for Dan Ford and Rod Carew, both of whom helped the Angels win their first American League West title in 1979. We did not have much pitching: Frank Tanana's arm had gone bad and Nolan Ryan was 16–14.

Jim Fregosi had done an excellent job as manager, and Don Baylor (.296, 36 home runs, 139 runs batted in), Bobby Grich (.294, 30 HR, 101 RBI), Dan Ford (.290, 21 HR, 101 RBI), and Brian Downing (.326, 12 HR, 75 RBI) had career seasons.

The opening game of the American League Championship Series against Baltimore was an omen. When Nolan Ryan left with a twinge in his leg and Grich dropped a pop fly, we should have known we were doomed. Ryan was our workhorse and Grich has always been one of the game's better fielders. We lost the series in four games.

After the series, Ryan became a free agent. He would never pitch another game for the Angels, which is one of my regrets in baseball. Gene Autry never interfered with decisions regarding player personnel, and in retrospect, I wish he had with Ryan.

I thought Ryan was simply asking for too much money, and Gene agreed. I wish he had overruled me. When Ryan signed with Houston for about $1.1 million a year, I thought it was too much.

A class man, Ryan had a special rapport with Anaheim fans. Nevertheless, he alone did not attract 10,000 people above our attendance average in the manner Koufax did for the Dodgers.

Ryan has five career no-hitters and undoubtedly he belongs in the Hall of Fame, but he was never much more than a .500 pitcher. And I've been criticized for saying so.

In 1979, Ryan's record was 16–14. I stated that to replace him, all we needed were two 8–7 pitchers. If nothing else, the mathematics bear that out. Ryan was 16–14 on a club that batted .282 with 164 home runs. Was that worth $1.1 million a year? I didn't think so.

By then, I began to realize that we weren't allowed to criticize players anymore. Long-term guaranteed

contracts had placed players above criticism. It
didn't matter that they'd be criticized only when they
weren't doing their jobs.

Based on a harmless comment I made with tongue
firmly in cheek, Don Baylor retired in 1981. He had
opened the season in a slump, with two hits in his
first 27 at-bats, a .074 average. Yet, he was featured
on the cover of the Angels' scorebook, in a picture
with Fred Lynn and Rod Carew.

"What's Don doing in that picture with those two
hitters?" I said to John Hall, a columnist for the
Orange County Register. When Hall printed the remark in his column the following day, Baylor retired.

He came into my office with tears in his eyes, he
was so mad. "What are you trying to do, humiliate
me?" he asked.

"No," I said. "It was said as a joke. Forget it."

"I'm not going to forget it. I'm going to quit."

"When?"

"Now."

What could I say? If he was going to quit, so be it.
When you lose Roberto Clemente, and Sandy Koufax
retires on you after winning 27 games, Don Baylor
quitting with an .074 batting average was not going
to make you panic.

He actually left the stadium. When he returned, he
met with Fregosi, who persuaded him to end his
"retirement." I knew he wouldn't quit, anyway. He
must have called Marvin Miller, the leader of the
Players Association, and Marvin explained it to him:
if he had missed one day, he wouldn't have been a 10-
year man.

I thought the remark was funny, and so did everyone else. I never realized it would create such a stir.
I guess it would have been funnier if I'd said it about
someone other than Don, whom I do like. He's a fine
man, an excellent leader, and someday he'll probably

be a quality major-league manager.

Sometimes, however, Baylor takes his leadership role among the players too seriously. In 1983, he testified on behalf of an outfielder, Bobby Clark, in Clark's salary arbitration hearing. Clark was seeking a $66,000 raise, despite the fact he had batted just .211 with eight runs batted in the year before. Clark was asking for $145,000 and we had submitted a figure of $105,000. In prior years, a .211 hitter would have had his salary cut, not raised.

Baylor's testimony included statements that Clark was the best young outfielder he'd seen come into the big leagues since he'd been playing. Consider, for a moment, the source: Baylor is a designated hitter because he is inadequate in the outfield. By no means should he have been called as an expert witness on a man's ability to play defense. Yet, his testimony helped Clark win the case.

Baylor is an impressive figure; when he talks, people listen. The abritrator listened, and we lost.

Now, consider Clark's career in the aftermath of the ruling that cost the Angels $40,000: he was traded to Milwaukee and, a year-and-a-half later, was sent to the minor leagues. Soon after that, he was out of baseball. How, in less than 1½ years, had he gone from being one of the best outfielders to come into the game in years to being a released minor-league player?

Baylor was clearly out of line in testifying on Clark's behalf. And the arbitrator, Charles Killingsworth, obviously knew little about the game of baseball. At one point in the hearing, Killingsworth even asked someone what the initials RBI stood for.

The biggest disappointment of my baseball career occurred in 1982 when the Angels failed to finish off the Milwaukee Brewers in the American League

Championship Series. We won the first two games in
Anaheim and needed only one victory in the next
three games in Milwaukee to provide Gene Autry
with his first champion since his horse by that name
had died.

We were carrying a 2-1 lead into the seventh
inning of the fifth and deciding game, when Luis
Sanchez served up a two-run single to Cecil Cooper.
We lost, 4-3. I was sick. This hurt far more than
losing the 13½-game lead in 1951.

After the first two games of the series, we simply
ceased playing well. The club let down and lost three
straight. I wanted that pennant more than I've
wanted anything else, for Gene Autry. He deserved
it.

In the aftermath of the '82 AL Championship
Series, Mr. Autry never said anything. He would not
second guess anyone, nor would he place blame. It
was not his style.

My association with Gene was one of the best of my
career. I thoroughly enjoyed working for him. I love
his contagious laugh. When Gene laughs, everyone
laughs with him. He has a great sense of humor.

He called for me one day, but I was not in the
office—I was getting a haircut. Let me explain that I
have a hairline that is rapidly receding.

"Where is he?" Mr. Autry asked my secretary,
Leslie Wilson.

"He's out getting a haircut," she replied.

"I'll hold," Mr. Autry said.

He is a remarkable person. In 1982, the players
retired the number 26 in Mr. Autry's honor, symbol-
izing the 26th man on the team. It was a genuine
expression of the way his players felt about him.

There is no better fan. To make the 200-mile round-
trip drive from Palm Springs to Anaheim every
night, he *has* to like the game. He sits there night

after night, watching the games closely and keeping a scorecard. Too often, the scorecard does not add up the way he would like. Nevertheless, he does not become disillusioned.

Gene is smart, too—he didn't make so much money because he was shy or stupid. When he has something to say, it behooves you to listen. I remember Gene standing and speaking at an owner's meeting years ago, when salary arbitration was merely in the discussion stage.

"Gentlemen," he said, "I've been in the entertainment business all my life, and the worst thing that can happen in baseball is for you to let these players go to arbitration." He told the owners to allow the players to go on strike before allowing them to take their cases to arbitrators. Not many of the owners understood Gene's thinking. They do now, after seeing several players receive raises—not salaries, but raises—of $600,000 through arbitration.

Gene doesn't say much at these meetings, but when he does have a point to make, you have to listen.

It's too bad that every GM does not have the opportunity to work with and for Gene Autrey. He is probably the only owner who would like his team to play a doubleheader every day.

15

Now Starring: Reggie, Rodney & Co.

People listened when the Cowboy sang, too. As an entertainer, Gene Autry was a superstar in his own right. He made records, he made movies, he made television shows, and he made money.

His own brilliant career was the impetus behind his insistence on signing or trading for stars. He knew the value of having recognizable names on the marquee. He knew what it would mean to the club to have names synonymous with baseball. When free agency first infested baseball, Autry signed Don Baylor, Bobby Grich, and Joe Rudi.

Myself, I'm against building a club through free agency. At heart, I'm a man who prefers building from within, through a strong minor league organization. It worked with the Dodgers, and it was beginning to work with the Padres, with the development of Dave Winfield, Randy Jones, Ozzie Smith, and Gary Lucas. And, too, it has started to work with the Angels with Wally Joyner, Kirk McCaskill, Mike

Witt, Dick Schofield, Jack Howell, and others.

The Angels are in competition with the Dodgers, which is why Mr. Autry invested so heavily in name players. We weren't competing with Detroit or Chicago or Cleveland. We competed with the Dodgers, who would take about $10 million from season-ticket sales to the bank in January. This was our competition.

We were competing for the entertainment dollar of Southern California baseball fans. If we were to put nine unknown youngsters on the field and try to compete with the Dodgers, we might just as well have folded our tent. Not many would pay to see the show.

Rod Carew and Reggie Jackson provided proof. When I joined the Angels in the winter of 1977, the club had sold 6,000 season tickets. We traded for Carew in February of 1979, and by opening day, we had sold 12,000 season tickets.

We signed Reggie in January of 1982. By opening day, our season-ticket count had risen to 18,000. Reggie and Rodney had paid for themselves before ever playing a game.

Carew made me realize that our fans in Orange County wanted players with whom they could relate, with whom they were familiar. This was the reason we went after established stars, without regard to the cost.

Reggie, Rodney, and Fred Lynn were the three most prominent players we acquired during my tenure with the Angels. In 1982, we had four former American League Most Valuable Players on the same club, the three aforementioned along with Don Baylor.

Of the three for whom I was responsible, the Angels got their money's worth from two of them, Jackson and Carew. On Lynn, we made a costly mistake, though at the time we thought otherwise. In fact, on the day we traded for Lynn in 1981, Baylor said, "We just won the pennant."

We bestowed a $5.2 million contract on a player who, by choice, was not a full-time player. In the four years we had Lynn, he missed virtually a full season, based on what can be construed as a full season for him. He missed 34 of 110 games in the strike-shortened 1981 season, 24 games in 1982, 45 games in 1983, and 20 games in 1984. Altogether, he missed 123 games.

Fred Lynn has all the talent in the world. Damn, he's got talent! But talent without desire is a waste of a gift. If Lynn had the intestinal fortitude of a Don Zimmer or a Brian Downing, he would unquestionably be one of the best players ever to wear a uniform. I remember when Roger Craig was still pitching. Every time he threw the ball, tears would come to his eyes, it hurt him so much. That's what I call intestinal fortitude. I question whether Lynn has it.

Lynn can run, he can throw, he can field, he can hit, and he can hit with power. Willie Mays and Mickey Mantle had the same attributes. So did Duke Snider. Those three are in the Hall of Fame. Lynn has Hall of Fame ability, but he must learn how to use it.

Fred came to us with a tarnished reputation. In Boston, he had already been accused of being a malingerer. When we made the trade that brought Fred to Anaheim, the Boston people told me that if we could get him to play, we'd have an exceptional player on our hands. To us, it was worth the risk. Unfortunately, not every gamble is a winner.

When you pay a player more than $1 million a year, you have a right to expect that player to participate in at least 140 games, barring serious injury. I was amused to read in the Angels' 1981 media guide a quote by Lynn: "My main goal is to play 162 games. If I can stay healthy, I know I can have the type of year everyone expects me to have."

Lynn needed two seasons to play 162 games.

One spring in Arizona, Lynn could not take batting practice one day because he had sprained his right wrist. Later that same day, he was seen playing tennis. Lynn plays tennis right-handed.

Suspiciously, the majority of Lynn's nagging injuries occurred when the opposition was starting a left-handed pitcher, notably a quality left-hander. At one point in the '83 season, Lynn had not started 18 times. In 13 of those 18 games, a left-hander had started for the Angels' opponent.

I had had enough. I told some newspapermen, "If there were 800 left-handers in the league, Fred Lynn might never play. I'm going to talk with him when he gets back to see if he knows his contract requires him to play against left-handed pitchers."

After the 1984 season, Gene Autry was interested in re-signing Lynn, but he eventually signed with the Baltimore Orioles. Gene called him to wish him well, but Fred wasn't in. Gene left his private number with Fred's wife, and asked her to have him call. He never did.

He had an excuse, of course. He told Angels vice president Mike Port that, "I didn't want to bother him." Bother him? Did Fred not wonder why Mr. Autry had left his private number if he did not want to be bothered?

Lynn took his reputation with him to Baltimore and lived up to it. In 1986, he missed 40 games. Midway through the 1986 season, Thomas Boswell wrote in the *Washington Post*:

. . . On June 27, (Lynn) returned after a 17-game absence because of a sprained ankle and flu. Last season, Cal Ripken had a badly sprained ankle and missed one game—an exhibition against Navy.

Lynn has missed more games with minor injuries in a season and a half with the Orioles (60) than Ripken and Eddie Murray have missed in their entire careers—a span of almost 2,500 games. Yet Lynn is the highest-paid Oriole—$1.35 million.

Lynn only plays when he feels perfect. Firemen go into burning buildings for $25,000 a year, but Lynn won't go into center field for $8,333.33 a day if his ankle hurts. Asked recently to pinch-hit with the bases loaded, Lynn said he didn't feel up to it.

A potentially serious injury is one thing. But sore ankles and sore throats are the things pros play through; that distinguishes them from amateurs who play for fun, not for a living.

We did not make a mistake when we signed Reggie Jackson to a four-year contract in January 1982. The best compliment I can pay Reggie is that he is perhaps the only player from the 1982 Angels who had the personality and intensity to be member of the 1955 Brooklyn Dodgers.

I had nearly signed Reggie five years earlier, after the 1976 season, when he became a free agent for the first time. I was still with the Padres, then. I had gone to New York to meet with him, as had Ray Kroc. I thought we had a deal worked out, for something in the vicinity of $500,000 per year. I had to return to San Diego for a meeting, and in the meantime, something happened. To this day, I don't know what it was, but Reggie has said that had I remained in New York, he probably would have signed with the Padres.

When Jackson became a free agent again, my son Peter, who is close to Reggie, told me we had a chance to get him if we were willing to spend a significant

amount of money. I asked Peter to tell Reggie we
were interested.

The Dodgers had just won the World Series in 1981
and competition was fierce. The Angels again needed
a marquee name who could sell tickets as well as
produce on the field. "How about somebody like
Jackson?" Mr. Autry suggested.

"Fine, if it's all right with you," I said.

"Go get him." That was all it took. This is the way
Gene operates. If he wants something, he says to go
after it.

It was my own personal philosophy not to negotiate
with a free agent until I was assured that player
would not be returning to his former team. I said to
Yankees owner George Steinbrenner, "George, unless
you tell me you're not interested, I'm not going after
him."

About a week later, George said he did not want to
re-sign him. "I would rather you sign him," Steinbrenner said to me, "because I don't want that Baltimore club to get him."

I flew to Phoenix to meet with Jackson's agent and
friend, Gary Walker, a fine young man who is now the
athletic director at Northern Arizona University. All
I wanted to know was whether Reggie was interested
in coming to Anaheim. Anaheim is not Los Angeles
and it is not New York. I wanted to know if he could
be happy in a smaller community.

Walker said Reggie would be happy any place he
could get along with his employers, notably Gene
Autry and me. After working for Steinbrenner for
five years, that was apparently an important
consideration.

Jackson, Walker, and Jackson's attorney met with
Gene and me, and we came to a tentative agreement.
One stumbling block was contract length. He wanted
five years and we said no. Jackson and Mr. Autry

went for a walk, by themselves, and when they returned, Jackson had agreed to a four-year contract, with an option for a fifth year. The option was ours.

It was Walker's idea to have an attendance clause inserted into the contract. Should the Angels' attendance skyrocket with the addition of Jackson, Walker said, Reggie should get a piece of the action. We had no objections to that. We gave him 50 cents for every ticket sold over 2.4 million, and he earned $203,680 from his attendance clause in 1982 when the Angels drew 2,807,360 fans.

They also wanted a bonus for Jackson in the event the Angels reached the playoffs. This was out of the question. Baseball is a team game. Had we agreed to this clause, it would signify to the rest of the players that Reggie did it by himself. Imagine the unrest *that* might have caused. Besides, we had reached the playoffs in 1979 without Reggie. His people understood.

For the first month of the season, Jackson looked as bad as George Steinbrenner looked good in letting Reggie leave New York. It was not an auspicious beginning. He did not hit his first home run until April 27.

The fans who did not like Reggie relished the opportunity to voice their displeasure. We had about 18 fans who bought box seats down the right-field line for the sole purpose of booing Jackson. Like him or not, though, he was great for business.

Jackson's first home run as an Angel was a memorable one. It came in Yankee Stadium, of all places, off Rod Guidry, of all people, and it helped the Angels defeat the Yankees, 3-2, before a crowd of 35,446 who chanted "Steinbrenner Sucks" after Reggie's homer.

All in all, it was a splendid association. Reggie has been good for the Angels, who have been good for Reggie. He did everything expected of him and more.

No one expected him to lead the league in home runs, yet in 1982, he tied Gorman Thomas for the American League lead with 39.

Reggie has the flair. He knows when the red light is on the camera. He does the right thing at the right time. In his inimitable way, he has been great for the game. He does the unexpected and people love it or loathe it, but they seldom ignore it.

He can be a Jekyll and Hyde. He can be the nicest young man you would ever want to meet one moment, and a pain in the rear the next. If you treat Reggie the way Reggie wants to be treated, he's a fine person. If you try to push him around or belittle him, he gets his back up.

I'm a Reggie man. I've always gotten along with him. He calls Evit and me once in a while just to say hello. Reggie, amazingly, loves to talk about baseball, and has time to do so. He has so many other things on his mind, particularly the outside interests that earn him more money than baseball does. Nevertheless, he will sit down and talk baseball, and talk about it sensibly. He knows how to play the game, no doubt about it.

On the field, Jackson is a hard-nosed player, which is why I say he could have been a member of the '55 Dodgers. He has ability, plus the desire to succeed. On ground balls, Jackson runs to first at top speed without fail, even though his top speed is not what it used to be. I never really saw much of him when he was in his prime, when he could play the outfield, run the bases, and throw. But people who saw him say he was more than adequate in every aspect of the game.

Reggie has expressed a desire to own a major league team, though I doubt it will ever happen. I think he's too smart. If you're going to spend the money necessary to operate a baseball club, you're better off putting it in the bank. Take Gene Autry, for instance. If he cared only about making money, he could sell the Angels tomorrow and put the $60 million in the bank at 10 percent interest.

Making money is a hobby of Reggie's. I can't see him spending his money on a business without any guarantees. But whatever Reggie decides to do after he has called it a career, he will undoubtedly do it flamboyantly.

The game will miss Reggie Jackson.

The game should miss Rod Carew, too. I know I will. The trouble with Rod was that he was suspicious of everyone, particularly the press. Maybe he had a right to be suspicious of the press, I don't know. The media never really treated Rod as a future member of the Hall of Fame. Then again, that may have been a by-product of how he treated the media. It probably worked both ways.

At any rate, Carew's reputation preceded him to Anaheim. "He doesn't drive in runs" and "he doesn't hit any home runs" were criticisms I often heard and read. Neither did Eddie Stanky or Pete Rose. Many quality hitters failed to drive in a lot of runs.

Rod was not paid to hit for power, anyway. He was paid to hit .300, which he did in all but his last two years with the Angels. When Carew does not bat .300, he isn't of much use to a club, which is probably why the Angels chose not to renew his contract after the 1985 season.

In the past few years, I've lost some respect for Rod Carew. When he first faced free agency, after the 1983 season, he said some derogatory things about the club based on the fact that he wished to be paid what he had earned in 1983. He earned more than $1 million in 1983, and we weren't about to pay him that again in 1984.

We allowed Carew to enter his name in the free

agent re-entry draft. Not one club selected him. For some reason, no one in baseball wanted a man who had hit .339 the year before. For that matter, we weren't interested, either. Nevertheless, we signed him to a two-year, $1.6 million contract. Do you know why? Mr. Autry felt he had an obligation to him.

When that two-year contract had expired, the Angels again were not interested in signing him. Neither was anyone else—Carew did not get so much as one offer. Then he inexplicably popped off about how the club did nothing in the way of honoring him for retiring. He said he had wanted to go out the way Carl Yastrzemski did, with a day in his honor and such.

Here's the catch: at no time did Carew tell the Angels he was retiring. He still wanted to play. He was miffed because the Angels did not throw him a retirement party. Never mind that he didn't intend to retire.

When the San Francisco Giants made him a token offer in May of 1986, Carew finally elected to announce his retirement, after which the Angels planned a day in his honor.

No one was immune to Carew's wrath, not even the one man who stood by him for years, Gene Mauch, his manager in Minnesota and with the Angels. Carew blasted Mauch for allegedly reneging on a promise to make phone calls on his behalf in an attempt to convince another team he could still play.

Again, Carew was suspicious of everyone. Ultimately, it may affect his getting voted into the Hall of Fame on the first ballot. It shouldn't, but it might. Writers don't have short memories. And Carew may have alienated himself from enough of those members of the Baseball Writers Association of America (who vote on the Hall of Fame) to prevent his election on the first ballot.

It would not be without precedent. It took Duke Snider 10 years to get into the Hall of Fame. Why would he make it 10 years after he was eligible rather than the first year? He certainly hadn't improved with time.

Funny thing about Rod Carew. Despite his suspicious nature, he is a fine person. He and his lovely wife, Marilynn, both are. I don't recall Rod ever turning down my request for him to do anything for the club off the field. He was always available and willing to do whatever he could to help.

16

Voices and Verses: The Media

Bob Hunter, then of the *Los Angeles Herald-Examiner*, and I were flying into Washington, D.C., to attend the winter meetings in Baltimore, when we passed over the Potomac River.

"I've never been to Washington in my life," Hunter said.

"Look, there's the Potomac," I said.

"Where! Where!" he said excitedly. I knew I had him hooked.

"Bob, see that spot right there? See where that big monument is? That's where Washington stood when he threw that silver dollar across the river."

"No kidding?" he said.

"Yeah. As a matter of fact, my great-, great-grandfather found that dollar. I still have it."

"No kidding?" he said again.

I was putting him on and he realized it, though he did not let on until his paper came out the next day.

He had written what I had said, making me look foolish. He wrote it to teach me a lesson.

The lesson is that you had better be careful what you say to the media. The media can be friend or foe, or both. My theory was always, respect the writers and they will respect you.

I never had too many problems with the media. In New York, it was fun, because the writers were all fans. When I came to Los Angeles, I could not have had a better relationship than I had with Bob Hunter, Frank Finch, Charlie Park, and John B. Old. They were all great guys. So were Phil Collier and Jack Murphy in San Diego.

Dick Young is the best baseball writer I have ever known. Bob Hunter is the hardest-working writer. Phil Collier is the most knowledgeable. Jack Murphy, a columnist for the *San Diego Union*, was a good friend and a brilliant writer. You could put Dink Carroll of the *Montreal Gazette* into the same category.

But of all the newspapermen I've known, I'd have to put Jim Murray of the *Los Angeles Times* in a class by himself. I have the utmost respect for him. His writing ability is without peer. He can make you laugh and he can make you cry, and no one would blame him if he did more of the latter in his personal life.

I've known Jim for a number of years and I know all that he's been through, including the loss of his dear wife. I could not have endured the heartaches he has had to endure and still retained my sense of humor. Yet, I've never seen him without a smile on his face, never. To me, that's remarkable. He must have had plastic surgery to affix that smile permanently on his face. He is an amazing man.

I like to have fun with the writers on occasion. During the season in 1983, when we were negotiating to re-sign Rod Carew, a writer wrote that I had not even met face-to-face with Carew's agent, Jerry Simon, who, in fact, had been in the office the day before. I called the writer the next day and said, "If that wasn't Simon in my office yesterday, who was it? Garfunkel?"

In my New York days, we used to have fun with the writers on the trains. One day, Mike Gavin, covering the Dodgers for the *New York Journal-American*, cut an artery in his hand and was bleeding profusely. We took him off the train in Boston so he could get medical help.

He could not cover the game that night, so Harold Parrott, our road secretary, wrote the story for him and put Mike's name on it. When I heard what Harold had done, I sent Mike a telegram that said, "Great story. Keep it up. Best story you ever did."

I had it signed Max Kase, his editor's name.

In retrospect, the most enjoyable writers to read were those who were critical. Bill Corum, one of the finest men who ever lived, was one of the most boring writers I've ever read. He never wrote anything nasty about anyone, and it became tiresome after awhile.

Dick Young was critical when necessary, but he was also fair. This fact was once overlooked by pitcher Clem Labine. One day, Labine had pitched himself into a jam, and he loaded the bases. Charley Dressen went out to the mound to talk with him. Charley had barely crossed the foul line on his way back to the dugout, when the ball landed in the center-field bleachers. Grand slam.

Young wrote what he and everyone else saw, that Labine's performance was pitiful. Sometimes the truth hurts, and Labine was hurt by what Dick had written.

The next day, I walked into the manager's office at Ebbets Field and heard screaming coming from the clubhouse. I went in and saw that Labine had Young by the throat.

"Get your hands off him," I yelled at Clem.

"Did you read what he wrote about me?" he said.

"Yes, I did, Clem. And for the last month I also read what he wrote on how great you have been. Dick didn't give up a home run into the center-field bleachers, you did."

He let go of Dick and apologized to him.

I was accused of deliberately nurturing a strong relationship with Young to keep him from writing derogatory stories about the Dodgers. It is a fallacy. When I was in Montreal and I'd visit New York, I didn't know many people there. If I wanted to go to a hockey game, Dick Young was right there with the tickets. Dick treated me as well when I was in the minor leagues as he did when I was in the major leagues. That's why I like Dick Young.

My initiation with California writers came in January of 1958, when I was living at the Townhouse in Los Angeles. At midnight one night, someone knocked on my door.

"Who is it?" I hollered.

"Frank Finch. I've got the biggest circulation west of the Mississippi. You've got to get up and have a drink with me."

I got up, got dressed, and went to the Zebra bar at the hotel to have a drink with Finch, of the *Los Angeles Times*. He was a great writer, a very literate writer, and he was, I would find out later, fun to be with.

We were in St. Louis once and the Dodgers were playing a doubleheader with the Cardinals. In the eighth inning of a tie game, we had a man on first and Duke Snider on third with one out. The batter hit the ball to the shortstop, who turned it into a double play. Snider, meanwhile, had not broken for home in an attempt to draw a throw there and prevent a double play. I was furious.

Harry Caray, the Cardinals' radio broadcaster, asked me to go on the air between games, and I agreed. I put the rap on Duke something terrible for failing to break for home.

The next day, John B. Old's paper, the *Los Angeles Herald*, had the story of me criticizing Duke. I was on the air in St. Louis; I had no idea how anyone back home had heard the broadcast.

Frank Finch, meanwhile, did not have the story, and his paper wanted to know why. As it turned out, Finch did not have it because he was where he was supposed to be, at the ballpark. For whatever reason, John B. Old had not left the hotel that day; he heard my interview on the radio in his room, and had a scoop.

In the spring of 1979, I was sitting with several writers in our press room at the Gene Autry Hotel in Palm Springs, and the subject was Howard Cosell. Everyone had an opinion on Howard, most of them derogatory. I began laughing.

"Why are you laughing?" I was asked.

"Because you people are doing exactly what ABC wants you to do. You're not talking about Vin Scully. You're not talking about Mel Allen. You're not talking about Red Barber. You're talking about Howard Cosell."

In my opinion, Howard Cosell did for football what the Catholic Church Index does for book sales. When the Catholic Church lists a book in its Index, it is instructing you not to read the book. Of course, everybody then buys the book to find out why they shouldn't read it. It becomes a bestseller.

Every week, newspapermen were criticizing Howard Cosell. More was written on Howard than on any other man or woman in the industry. Most of it was negative. As a result, those who weren't football fans would turn on Monday Night Football to find out for themselves what was wrong with Howard Cosell. The audience would grow, the ratings would increase, and ABC loved it.

I was never a big football fan before Howard Cosell became a fixture on Monday Night Football. I tuned in so I could see for myself what all the fuss was about. Now, I miss Cosell on Monday Night Football. I imagine that Monday Night Football misses Howard, too.

One of Howard's biggest critics had always been Dick Young, first of the *New York Daily News* and later of the *New York Post*. Dick and I have been friends for 40 years. Still, I don't understand why he is so critical of Howard. When Dick was younger, he was exactly like Howard. He told it as it was.

I don't think Howard cares when people abuse him or write negative articles about him. I'm sure he probably relishes the attention. There can be no debate about one point though—he is unique.

I knew Howard Cosell when he carried a 40-pound tape recorder around. You would be sitting around the lobby of a hotel, having a conversation with someone, and Howard would come over and turn on the tape recorder. Then he'd go to his room, edit it, and come back to ask whether he could use it. Then he'd go out and sell it. But he would never use it without receiving permission first.

When I was with the Padres in the early seventies, we were searching for a radio broadcaster. At the time, we had a working agreement with the Hawaii Islanders of the Pacific Coast League.

Their broadcaster sent us tapes of his work and he

was fine, except for one small detail. He sounded too much like Vin Scully. Showing no foresight whatsoever, we politely turned him down.

His name was Al Michaels, and today he is one of the finest, most respected broadcasters in the business.

One of my first assignments as vice president of the Dodgers was also one of my toughest. Vin Scully had begun broadcasting Dodger games in 1950, and I was to decide whether to renew an option to rehire him for the 1951 season.

We wanted Scully back, but his ability was not the problem. We still had the popular Red Barber at the time, and we did not want to hurt his feelings. I also knew that had we asked Red's opinion, he'd have said yes, with tough limitations.

What I did was ask Walter O'Malley to let the ad agency that sponsored the broadcasts decide. Its representative, Tom Valenti, said, "You've got to be crazy. Keep Scully." He was Scully's biggest booster.

Of course, we could not fire Barber. He was a star. I remember one time we were playing a split doubleheader that began in the morning. Brooklyn had a million people within walking distance of Ebbets Field, but by 15 minutes before game time, only 5,000 were in the park. Red went on the air and told the audience, "We'll hold the game up 15 minutes, and we have plenty of good seats left, so come on out."

Forty minutes later, we had about 27,000 people.

We elected to retain Scully, which, in retrospect, was one of the best decisions the club ever made. What would the Dodgers have been without Scully?

With him, they were a remarkable success. More than anyone, Scully made the Dodgers successful in Los Angeles. He was the biggest asset we had coming to California. Number one, he taught people how to watch baseball games. Number two, he got women interested in the Dodgers, and if you do that, you're going to be successful. A husband might go to a game once a week, but he is not going twice a week without his wife's consent. Therefore, if you don't get women interested, you might not be as successful.

After the Dodgers had been in Los Angeles for two years, Scully probably could have been elected mayor. He was that popular. He has a way about him that makes you love both him and the club. People in Los Angeles are fans of Scully almost as much as they are fans of the Dodgers.

I have often wondered whether we would have been as successful had we not had Scully in the broadcast booth. I doubt it.

Since I retired, Scully and Joe Garagiola have made my Saturdays enjoyable. I've never really had the chance to watch the Game of the Week before, but now I look forward to spending my summer Saturday afternoons with Vin and Joe.

17

Let's Make a Deal: Negotiations

Money was scarce many times during my career, particularly during our early years in San Diego. We had to hustle for every dollar then. Every time we got a player with any value, we would sell him. In one short span in the early seventies, I sold Al Santorini to St. Louis, Al Ferrara to Cincinnati, and Ed Spiezio to the Chicago White Sox.

Then my phone rang.

"Am I next?" the voice on the other end asked before hanging up. It was my mother calling from Florida. She was 81 at the time.

I immediately phoned her back.

"What's the matter?" I said.

"Well, you sold three Italians in a row," she said. "I figured I was next."

When it comes to player personnel, even your own mother second-guesses you. For the most part, it is a can't-win situation, be it a trade, signing a free agent, or simply negotiating a contract. No matter what you do, someone will be angry with you. It's the nature of the business.

Trading is an area in which you leave yourself open to the greatest amount of second-guessing. To me, a trade should not be judged until a season ends, at which time you have statistics and standings to show how a player helped the team.

At any rate, trading is a lost art form. Too many factors enter into a trade today, making the process difficult. You have agents and lawyers involved; you have long-term contracts to consider; you have no-trade clauses in contracts; you have to ask whether the players involved are suspected of using drugs.

Trades used to be made on handshakes, but those days ended in the seventies. At the winter meetings one year, Joe McDonald and Bob Scheffing of the Mets agreed to send pitcher Craig Swan to the Angels in exchange for rookie shortstop Dickie Thon. We shook hands on the deal.

Then Mrs. Vincent deRoulet, the owner of the Mets, came in and said she would not make the trade, that it was off.

"There's no way I'm going to give up a 30-year-old for a 20-year-old boy," she said. It was a silly statement to make. So I offered to give her the oldest player on our club.

McDonald and Scheffing were embarrassed. When you shake hands with men like them, you know that you've consummated a deal. But there was nothing they could do. Mrs. deRoulet owned the club. It was the first time in my career that someone had reneged on a deal.

In August of 1982, we acquired Tommy John from the Yankees for a minor-league player to be named later. We gave the Yankees a list of players, and they selected pitcher Dennis Rasmussen. I called Dennis and told him he was going to the Yankees, though not right away. He was excited.

A month later, Yankees' owner George Steinbrenner decided he did not want Rasmussen. That
was okay by me. I told him to choose from the other
three players on the original list.

Then I called Rasmussen to explain that he
wouldn't be going to the Yankees after all, that,
luckily for us, and unhappily for him, the Yankees
had decided to take someone else.

"But you'll get every shot to make the Angels," I
explained to him. He understood.

A short time after that, Bill Bergesch, the Yankees'
vice president in charge of player personnel, called
and said, "George changed his mind again. He wants
Dennis Rasmussen."

"I can't do that now," I said. "I've already told him
he's coming to training camp with the Angels. And
George had called and said he didn't want him."

"Well, George has changed his mind," Bill said.

"I don't care whether George has changed his mind
or not. He's not going to get him."

End of conversation. Later, Bergesch called me
back.

"Buzzie, George called me in and said if we don't
get Rasmussen, I'm fired," Bill said.

"Bill, there's no ballplayer in the world that is
worth a friend of mine getting fired. You can have
Rasmussen."

That's how George worked.

Steinbrenner, by the way, can also be a very
generous man, to which all his ex-managers can
attest. He's made them all wealthy. At an American
Association dinner in 1978, I was sitting between
Harold Cooper, the president of the Association, and
Steinbrenner. Harold mentioned that the league was
having a financial problem and that it needed
another umpire.

"How much would that cost?" Steinbrenner asked.

"About $20,000," Cooper replied.

"Forget about it," Steinbrenner said. "You've got it."

Another time, I was visiting George Sisler, Jr., the president of the Yankees Columbus club in Columbus, Ohio. Sisler took me through their fine stadium and into the training room, which had better equipment than most major league clubs. It was all donated by Steinbrenner, to the tune of $50,000.

Sometimes I wonder whether integrity is a dying trait. Today, it is caveat emptor, let the buyer beware. It is a hallmark of the modern era. It isn't that the people operating clubs are dishonest, it's just that the competition is so great in baseball these days. You have to use whatever means are available to field a winner.

I'm often afraid that were I still in baseball today, I might try to con my son Peter, the president of the Cleveland Indians, into taking somebody who could not help him.

In 1981, we signed pitcher Bill Travers to a four-year, $1.5 million contract. He never won a game for the Angels. When we got him, he had arm problems. Those who knew he wasn't healthy did not tell us. Of course, they had no reason to tell us, because we hadn't asked.

Still, that would not have happened 20 or 30 years ago. If something was wrong with a player, you were told. There was a rule then stipulating that if, within 10 days after acquiring a player you learned he was injured or he failed to report, you could return his contract.

Case in point:

When I was with the Dodgers, we made a deal to send pitcher Jack Smith to the Cubs for a catcher. It turned out that the catcher could not play due to injury. They took him back. Do you know who they sent us instead? Jim Brewer. He saved 14 games for the Dodgers in 1968.

A good trade is one in which you give up very little and get a player who helps. Often, it is better to be lucky than to have a lengthy scouting report.

Another case in point:

In spring training in 1960, the Cubs wanted to acquire shortstop Don Zimmer from us. They asked what it would take to get Zimmer. I said $27,500 and three players, and, to my surprise, they agreed. I asked them which three players they had in mind.

The first two were Lee Handley, an outfielder, and Johnny Goryl, a second baseman. I agreed to take both of them. They offered Ben Johnson and Moe Thacker, both of whom I rejected. Then they suggested Ron Perranoski, a left-handed pitcher coming out of the Army.

"Perranoski?" I said. "I don't want Perranoski. Who is he?" I had never heard of him.

"We gave him $30,000," they interjected quickly.

If the Cubs had given him $30,000 to sign, he might be worth something.

"OK," I said, "I'll take him. I'll take $27,500 and those three players."

I later sold Goryl for $25,000 and Handley for $10,000, giving us $62,500 and Ron Perranoski for Zimmer. Perranoski, a pitcher I took on a lark, became one of the best relief pitchers in baseball. He was 16-3 with 21 saves for the 1963 Dodgers.

When I went to say goodbye to Zimmer, incidentally, I asked him how he was fixed for money.

"I've got four dollars," he said. He wasn't to get paid until the 15th of the month, so I reached into my pocket, grabbed all the money I had there, and gave it to him. Fifty dollars.

Melvin Durslag, the respected columnist of the *Los Angeles Herald-Examiner*, had witnessed this scene.

"That's the nicest thing I've ever seen anybody do," he said later.

"What are you talking about?" I asked.

"You saw the kid didn't have any money and you gave him all the money you had."

"Mel," I said, "when I went in there, I had $300. I put $250 in this pocket and $50 in this pocket. I gave him $50. I knew he'd take the entire $300 otherwise."

I traded Zimmer twice. I traded pitcher Bob Miller three times and kept getting him back for nothing. I traded Tommy Lasorda twice and got him back, each time at a profit.

When we had no money and few players at San Diego, people would give me ballplayers. One day I mentioned to my friend Spec Richardson, the general manager of the Houston Astros, that we needed pitching.

"I've got a pitcher here who isn't even going to make our club," he said. "I'll let you have him."

"Who?"

"Danny Coombs, a left-hander. He ought to be able to help."

"Fine," I said.

"How much will you give us for him?"

"I don't have any money, you know that."

"What do you mean?"

"Come on. Just send him to me."

"Well, I've got to put something down on the paper."

He put down $50,000 as the purchase price for Danny Coombs. He signed the papers, sent them to the commissioner to be signed, and they came to me to be signed.

An assistant to the commissioner called me 30 days after the deal was made to remind me that the $50,000 was due. Spec, meanwhile, understood that I wasn't going to pay anything.

Fortunately, there was a post office strike in New York at the time.

"I don't want to take the chance sending the check for $50,000 to New York because of the strike," I told the man. "The check might get lost in the mail. Is it all right if I send it directly to Spec?"

"Sure," he said. Of course, I never sent the check.

I had the opportunity to talk trade with Casey Stengel once, and it was an experience I'll never forget. Casey was one of the most remarkable characters in baseball. Anyone who knew him had to love him—not necessarily understand him, but just love him.

At the winter meetings one year, I was getting in the elevator about midnight when Casey confronted me.

"You're just the man I want to see," he said. "Come here." He grabbed me by the arm and took me into one of the anterooms.

We sat down, and he began talking about this big, big, strong fellow who could help us, this strong right-handed hitter with power. He talked for two hours.

"I think we can make this deal," he said finally.

"Fine. Let's make the deal, Casey," I said.

"Fine. We'll take Fred Kipp."

"Let me think about it."

I went back to my room, got in bed, and started laughing. I had been with Casey, listening to him talk about this big right-handed hitter who was going to help us win the pennant. In those two hours, he never told me the guy's name. That was Casey. I later learned he was talking about Gus Triandos.

A classic example of how some deals were made is the time we sent Andy Pafko to the Milwaukee

Braves before the 1953 season. Pafko was from Wisconsin, and the Braves had just moved to Milwaukee from Boston. So they wanted Pafko, a man with whom Milwaukee fans could identify.

John Quinn, the general manager of the Braves, came to my room about 6 o'clock one night at the winter meetings. The talk came around to Pafko.

"We'll give you $75,000 for him," Quinn said.

"No, you can't have him," I said.

About 9 P.M., John said, "We'll give you $100,000 for him."

"No," I said. It got later and later and we were still talking. By 11 P.M. the offer for Pafko had risen to $125,000.

"You know that I have to have a player in the deal if I do that, for tax purposes," I said.

He said he'd give us $125,000 and Roy Hartsfield for Pafko.

"I don't think so," I said. It was about midnight and I was getting tired. I got up and went into the bedroom and John followed me.

"I'll tell you what we'll do," John said. "We'll give you $150,000 and Roy Hartsfield. That's it."

I put my pajamas on and got into bed.

"I can't go more than $150,000," he said.

I was in bed and suddenly John was taking off his clothes. He took his shirt off, then his pants.

"What are you doing?" I said.

"I'm going to get in bed with you until you give me Pafko."

"You've got him, right now," I said, and the deal was made.

When I was with the Brooklyn Dodgers, the prohibitive cost of operating a spring training camp for the Dodgers and 27 minor-league clubs made it necessary for us to sell enough players each year to ensure a profit.

The best source of income was Bill Veeck, then of the St. Louis Browns. At the time, I doubt that Bill had $10 in the bank, but somehow he paid every dollar he owed the Dodgers for the players he purchased, about $300,000 total.

One spring, we sold Jim Gentile to Veeck's White Sox for $75,000 but Gentile himself vetoed the deal by staying out long beyond curfew that night.

I went to his room in Vero Beach to tell him we had traded him to the White Sox, that he was going to the major leagues. He wasn't there. At 2 A.M., he still wasn't in his room.

The next morning, I called Bill Veeck and told him I was going to back out of the deal.

"No, you can't do that," he said.

"I have to. Everybody in this camp knows that this kid stayed out all night. If I sell him, they'll think, 'That's what you have to do to get sold to a big league club.' I'm not going to do it."

With Veeck's permission, the sale was called off. Gentile's penalty was that he spent another needless year in the minors when he could have been playing with the White Sox.

I sold several players to Paul Richards, too. I had one price for Paul: $50,000. That was what he paid at different times for Billy Loes, Preacher Roe, Billy Cox, and Dick Williams.

I acquired Joe Altobelli one year and loaned him to a friend running the club in Syracuse. Two weeks later, I saw in the paper that Altobelli had gotten two hits for the Minnesota Twins. I called Clark Griffith and said, "How'd you get him?"

"We bought him for $25,000," he said.

"That's my $25,000," I said.

I called my friend, who explained that he was going to ask my permission to sell Altobelli, but that he knew I wouldn't mind.

"How much did you get for him?"

"I got $7,500," he said.

"Mr. Griffith just told me he paid you $25,000."

With friends like that . . .

The Dodgers purchased Sal Maglie from Cleveland for $1,000, much to the chagrin of our fans. When Maglie was with the Giants, he was a Dodger beater and the fans hated him. When we acquired him, they wanted to run me out of town.

As it turned out, it was one of the better deals we ever made. At 39 years of age, Maglie won 13 games and pitched a no-hitter in 1956, helping the Dodgers win their second straight National League pennant.

Another superb deal we made was acquiring Jim Gilliam from the Baltimore Elite Giants. I was the general manager at Montreal at the time. Spencer Harris, a Dodger minor league executive, called to tell me the Elite Giants needed money and that I could buy some players at a discount.

For $11,000, I purchased Gilliam, Joe Farrell, and Joe Black. When I called Mr. Rickey, he was furious that I had spent $11,000 of his money.

"You did what?" he said when I told him. In the end, it proved to be a pretty shrewd deal.

Arguably the best deal the Dodgers ever made was in 1940, when Ted McGrew went to Louisville, scouted Pee Wee Reese, and recommended to Larry MacPhail that the Dodgers buy him from the Red Sox farm club for $75,000. You can't do much better than to acquire a Hall-of-Fame shortstop for $75,000.

One of the better trades of my later years was sending Dan Ford to Baltimore for third baseman Doug DeCinces. In 1982, DeCinces was as good an all-around third baseman as I'd ever seen.

DeCinces, incidentally, said early in 1985 that he was struggling because he was in the last year of his contract and it preyed on his mind. I found that amusing. I thought about Ted Williams and Joe DiMaggio and Duke Snider and Mickey Mantle and Willie Mays. Every year was the last year of their contracts because they never had anything but one-year contracts. Yet it never affected them. Why should it affect today's players?

For pressure, take the case of Fresco Thompson. In 1929, he had 202 hits and batted .324 with the Philadelphia Phillies, and took a pay cut in 1930. Why? Because he was only fourth on the team in batting. Lefty O'Doul hit .398, Chuck Klein hit .356, and Pinky Whitney hit .327.

Imagine batting .324 in the major leagues and taking a pay cut.

Contract negotiations were interesting before the advent of the agent and over-inflated salary figures. Marvin Miller, director of the Players Association, did a great job for the players. However, he didn't realize that GMs were doing the same kind of job for the owners.

Pee Wee Reese once said about negotiating with me that "We were like kids going into war with a pop-gun." It was no different with any other club. Baseball's reserve clause, which bound a player to a team for life, kept salaries within reason everywhere. So did the fact that excessive money simply was not available.

In fact, one of the few regrets I have in baseball is that I wasn't able to pay Drysdale, Koufax, Campanella, Erskine, Hodges, Gilliam, et al., the kind of money players are getting today. There was a reason for it, of course. We did not have it.

The price of a good seat at Ebbets Field was $2.50. We had no television package whatsoever, and income generated by radio was minimal. Our attendance dropped from 1.8 million to just over 1 million in five years. We did not have money to give away. And you cannot go to the bank to borrow money to pay players.

You would try to stay within a budget, but that was next to impossible. In Brooklyn, for instance, if we lost two games due to rain, that could be the difference between making and losing money. Or, if a player like Koufax or Newcombe won 27 games, you might have to pay him more than you had expected. So you did whatever you had to do to keep salaries down.

After Newcombe won 27 games for the Dodgers in 1956, he asked for a $35,000 contract for 1957.

"Newk," I said, "you won 27 games. If I give you $35,000, you'll get out there on the mound and start to think, 'Damn, I've got to win 27 games to get $35,000 again.' I don't want you to have that kind of pressure. I'll give you $30,000 and I don't care how many games you win."

He accepted it.

Chuck Connors once sent me a contract he signed in a most unusual way. I'll let him tell the story:

"Buzzie was the general manager in Montreal, and in 1948 we had a helluva club," Connors said. "I wasn't so sure of making it, but I did. We won the International League pennant, we won the playoffs, and we won the Little World Series. I was the all-league first baseman at the end of the season. I hit .307, drove in 108 runs, and had 19 or 20 home runs.

"After Christmas, I wrote Buzzie a letter in which I said I did this and I did that. I made $400 a month in 1948 and I wanted $500 or $600 a month in 1949. He wrote me back explaining why he couldn't do that. What I did was I dipped my pen in my own blood and signed the contract and told Buzzie, 'You want my blood, you've got it.' "

In 1958, we called up Bob Wilson, a pretty good hitter, to the big club. Over the winter, he was playing in Puerto Rico, where I sent him a contract for $1,000 a month, which was $6,000 for the season. The major-league minimum at the time was $5,000. Wilson called and said he wasn't going to sign for a penny less than the minimum. By his calculations, $1,000 a month came out to $4,000 a year. He wound up signing for $5,000.

That's why they need agents, I guess.

When we first came to Los Angeles, I asked Dick Walsh, my assistant for a while, to help me sign some of the younger players, including pitcher Danny McDevitt. Dick sent Danny a contract which he sent back shredded into a thousand pieces.

"How do you handle this?" Dick asked me.

"Here's what you do," I said. "Send the contract back to him just the way it is, in pieces, and send him another contract for $500 less. Tell him he can sign the one for $500 less and come to camp or he can paste the other one together and sign that."

McDevitt signed for $500 less.

Occasionally players would ask for less than they were worth or less than I had planned on paying. One was Gil Hodges. In 1956, he came in to sign his contract and he wanted $25,000. I wanted to give him more. But I couldn't give him more than he asked because it would set a precedent. Other players might expect more, too.

"Gil, you're a gambling man," I said. Hodges was a horseplayer. "I'm going to put five pieces of paper in a hat. I'm going to write $23,000 on one, then $24,000, $25,000, $26,000, and $27,000. There's three pieces of paper where you get what you want or more and two where you get less. That's a good gamble. Do you want to gamble?"

"All right," he said. He picked one and it was for $27,000. In fact, I had written $27,000 on all five slips of paper. To this day, God rest his soul, he thinks he outsmarted me.

One time I gave a player more than he asked, with a predictable result. If I did it for one player, others would expect the same treatment. The players involved were John Roseboro and Charlie Neal. Roseboro came in to talk contract and I asked him how much he wanted.

"I think I ought to get twelve-five," he said.

I asked my secretary Edna to make out a contract for $13,000, $500 more than Roseboro had asked. John left the office and I heard him talking to Charlie, who was waiting to come in to sign his contract. John was telling him how he'd asked for $12,500 and Buzzie had given him $13,000.

Charlie came in and I asked him how much he wanted.

"Thirteen thousand," he said, under the assumption I would then give him $13,500.

"Edna," I said, "bring in a contract for twelve-five."

When Neal left the office, I could hear him arguing with Roseboro. Charlie thought John had lied to him.

One year, I had signed Tommy Davis to a contract for $50,000. Ron Fairly was coming in to negotiate his contract, and I knew he was going to ask for far more than I felt he was worth. So I had a dummy contract drawn up. It showed that Tommy Davis would be paid $18,500. I put it on my desk, where it could be seen easily.

When Fairly came into the office, I came up with an excuse to leave for a minute. I knew Fairly would peek at the dummy contract. When he saw that Davis would make only $18,500, he figured he could not ask for more money than a National League batting champion was getting. Fairly signed for $18,500. However, the Dodgers made it up to Ron the following year.

I will say this about Ron. He was a man who never got the proper credit for being a pretty good player. An outfielder originally, he adapted to first base better than anyone I'd ever seen. He made the play to second base on a bunt better than most first basemen.

Incentive clauses, popular in today's contracts, were used in the past, too, though the rewards were considerably smaller. When Tommy Davis first came up, he was already a good hitter, but he liked to pull everything. So I made a deal with him: I would give him $100 for every hit he got to the right of second base. It cost me $3,500, but it made him a great hitter.

You could do things like that in those days. It was incentive. If you offered a ballplayer $100 for doing something today, he would laugh at you.

When we moved to California, the players were given leverage. The weather in California was better than the weather in the East. Players weren't as anxious to get to spring training as they were when they lived in New York.

Johnny Podres lived in Witherbee, New York, where in February it is cold. One year, he sent me a telegram saying, "Accept your terms. Be in Vero next week." I had not even sent him a contract. It was so cold, he couldn't wait to get to Florida.

In our never-ending search for the player who can make a difference, sometimes we overlook the obvious. This was the case in 1959, when, during midseason, it appeared we had a chance to win the National League pennant. What we needed most was a quality relief pitcher.

I had no idea where to look for one. I tried to trade for one, but that effort was futile. Finally, I called John Corriden, who was well into his 80s at the time.

He was doing some scouting for us in Indianapolis.

I asked John to scout every American Association team to come through Indianapolis to see if anyone had a relief pitcher who could help us.

A week later, John called and said he had found our man, and that we already had him. He was playing for our St. Paul farm club.

"Who?" I said, not believing him.

"Larry Sherry," John said.

"Are you sure?"

"What are you paying me to do? You're paying me to scout. Take him."

I knew of Sherry, but I did not think he was ready yet. I convinced John to take a second look. And his second opinion was the same as his first. On John's recommendation, we brought Sherry to the Dodgers.

In about half a season, Sherry was 7-2 with nine saves for the Dodgers, and we tied with Milwaukee for the National League pennant. Throughout the stretch drive, I called John almost every day to tell him how much I appreciated the job he had done.

In the first playoff game with Milwaukee, Sherry entered the game in the second inning and shut down the Braves the rest of the way. John was home watching the game on television.

Later, his wife called me.

"He was sitting there watching television and he asked me to get him a lollipop," she said, using John's term for a beer, "and when I brought it back, he was sitting in his chair very still."

Watching Sherry take the mound, John had died, undoubtedly a happy man.

18

Watching the Fun Set:
The Game Today

Baseball was once fun and games. Today it is only
games. I know the players are making millions now,
and, I suppose, some owners are, too. But there's not
a laugh in the millions.

Take George Steinbrenner, for instance. In 1979,
the volatile owner of the Yankees was irked about
scheduling he deemed unfair. For example, the Yankees had to play a doubleheader in Milwaukee one
day, then had to return to play in Yankee Stadium
the next day. When the Yankees failed to win the
pennant, Steinbrenner tried to place some of the
blame on the schedule.

Steinbrenner wanted to have Bob Holbrook, the
man in charge of scheduling, fired. George raised
hell with him.

I did not know George at the time, but I wrote him
a letter.

"Dear George," I wrote, "I think you're absolutely
right. Bob should be fired. It was a terrible schedule.

It probably did cost you the pennant. But keep in mind he's the same fellow who made out the schedule the previous year when you won the pennant. Did you give him a World Series ring for that?"

I received a two-page letter from Steinbrenner, explaining why Holbrook did not deserve a World Series ring. I had sent the letter as a gag, but Steinbrenner took it seriously.

George Steinbrenner does have a sense of humor, I'm sure, but he takes baseball so seriously, as does nearly everyone else these days. It has always been a business. The difference now is that it is big business. And in big business, there is no time for jocularity.

This is one of the problems with baseball today. The stakes have grown so great that competition, is fierce. It used to be that we, in baseball management, were in competition with each other, but we were also partners. Today, they're in competition, but they are not partners.

Corporations such as Seagrams, Anheuser-Busch, the Chicago Tribune Co., Turner Cable, and Domino's Pizza have replaced individual owners. Corporations care only about the bottom line.

To make money in baseball, teams have to win. To win, the clubs have to have the best players. To get the best players, they have to buy them. To buy them, they must outbid each other. The cycle is vicious, and it has hurt the game.

It is not easy to have sympathy for management, of which I was a part. Management blames the players for the position it finds baseball in today. It should look again. Not once did I see a player take an owner by the throat and say, "You have to give me this money."

If Ray Kroc or Gene Autry had come to me and said, "Buzzie, you're not to give any player more than $300,000" what would have happened? I surely wasn't going to pay them with my own money.

Ballplayers today think the world owes them a living. They are appalled when they go to a golf course and are asked to pay fees like the rest of us. I don't know of a modern player who does not want to be the richest man in the cemetery.

The free agent draft isn't of much use. A good farm system is a far better means by which to build a team, as the Orioles may have learned. In 1985, they signed Fred Lynn, Don Aase, and Lee Lacy. By 1986, they were a last-place club. They could have used three youngsters from their farm system, at a cost of $180,000, and done no worse.

Long-term contracts are another problem. In the era of one-year contracts, a player always had someone looking over his shoulder. If he played poorly or didn't play at all, he was released. Today, they can't release a player without eating an enormous guaranteed contract. Where is a player's motivation to play when he isn't feeling 100 percent? Where is his motivation to play well when he knows he'll be paid well next year and the year after, regardless?

Complacency is a by-product of the long-term contract. Players today generally do not play with the same desire and determination. In a way, it's understandable. It's human nature. Why should I be a Peter Reiser and run through a wall? I'm going to get paid anyway.

Then you see owners complaining about how much money they're paying their players, yet they're paying them anyway. Fernando Valenzuela of the Dodgers is getting a million-and-a-half. Maybe he deserves it, though I don't know anybody who is worth a million-and-a-half. To pay for that contract, an additional 300,000 tickets must be sold. No player can put 300,000 people in the stands by himself. To do so, Fernando would have to pitch 15 times at home and draw an additional 20,000 people each time he pitched. Since the Dodgers' season-ticket sales are at 27,000, the club would have to virtually sell out every time Fernando took the mound.

The mathematics here are crude; other factors are involved, and it isn't quite this simple. But the point is that it is impossible for Fernando Valenzuela to generate $1.5 million in income by himself, without help from his 23 teammates.

Then, too, there is the method by which salaries are determined. Raises used to be given on merit. Players earned them. Today, they're given on the basis of what another player with a similar number of years experience is earning. If some club is stupid enough to pay a player $1 million, why should others have to follow suit? Is stupidity contagious?

A standard player contract still stipulates that a salary can be cut up to 20 percent, or a total of 30 percent over two years. When was the last time you heard of a player taking a salary cut, save for an aging player attempting to hang on for another year or two?

Certain players are unaffected by long-term contracts and exorbitant salaries, of course. Pete Rose would play with the same determination no matter what. So would Reggie Jackson and Steve Sax. Eighty percent of the players probably would. It used to be 100 percent.

It is time baseball uses its hard head. Today, players must play three years before they're eligible for arbitration. Clubs should hold the salaries down for those years. What is the sense in giving $135,000 to a second-year player who made the major league minimum his rookie season? Raise him to $75,000 his second year and to $90,000 his third year.

If baseball did that, another problem would arise as a result, no doubt. Agents would protest, and would convince their clients to take measures that would only hurt the players themselves, such as holding out.

Agents may be the worst thing that has ever happened to baseball. It is a crime, really. When Dickie Thon was a rookie with the Angels, we planned to pay him the major league minimum, $20,000 at the time. He wanted $25,000. We said no. He hired an agent. He eventually signed for $21,000. After giving his agent his commission, Thon made less than the major league minimum.

Gary Pettis of the Angels lost his arbitration hearing in 1986, and as a result he made less money than he would have without an agent, by accepting the Angels' final offer before his case went to arbitration.

Agents who do more for their clients than negotiate a contract probably deserve what they get. Those who stay with a player and help him invest his money and generate outside income serve a purpose. Unfortunately, they are the exception. Most agents who make a lot of money these days work two months a year, November and December.

It isn't fair to baseball. This is why I would like very much to see the Players Association do something about it, though I doubt it will. What the Players Association should do is hire six young aggressive lawyers, pay them $100,000 each, and let them negotiate all the contracts as they come up for renewal. Hire more lawyers, if the workload calls for it. It should be noted first-year players and players with multi-year contracts wouldn't require the service of an agent.

The Players Association would have no trouble finding capable lawyers willing to earn $100,000 for working two months or so a year. Baseball, then, could save several million dollars on agents' commissions. The players' salaries would be the same (less the commissions), and baseball would have found an effective way to cut costs.

The way it works today is that an agent takes his cut, and the money is gone from baseball, never to come back. The agents aren't going to invest any money in baseball. When a player receives his money, he is at least providing entertainment for the public, albeit not always quality entertainment. Agents provide nothing.

It has gotten to the point where you can't even talk with a player anymore. A few years ago, Rollie Fingers's son was in the hospital. Rollie is a friend of mine, and I wanted to find out how his boy was. So I called, and Rollie wasn't there. I left a message.

Rollie didn't return my call. His agent did.

"What did you want?" the agent asked.

"I just wanted to know how his son is," I replied.

The agents have taken over.

After the 1984 season, I learned that pitcher Don Aase had agreed to sign with the Baltimore Orioles, though he had not yet informed the Angels' Mike Port. So I called Aase, simply to wish him the best.

"Congratulations," I said. "I understand you've signed with Baltimore."

Before I could finish what I had to say, he said, "I can't talk to you. You have to talk with my agent."

I mumbled something and hung up. Incredible.

Aase's signing with Baltimore was unethical, to say the least. Aase and Fred Lynn, both former Angels who signed with Baltimore after the 1984 season, are represented by Jerry Kapstein.

An Oriole scout let it be known that the Orioles were about to sign Lynn to a five-year contract with the stipulation that they must also sign Aase, an Angel relief pitcher. It was not a problem. Both players were represented by Kapstein. It was unethical, which I pointed out to both the commissioner and Hank Peters, the general manager of the Orioles.

Keep in mind, it was no fault of the agent—he was just doing his job. The fault lay with the Orioles.

Baltimore, in fact, negotiated with four free agents, although teams are permitted to sign only three. Besides Lynn and Aase, they also negotiated with Lee Lacy and Andre Thornton. In so doing, they drove up the price of all four players.

If baseball is trying to save money, it has a funny way of going about it. By negotiating with four free agents, all the Orioles did was raise the price the Cleveland Indians would have to pay to re-sign Thornton.

One way to save money, at least in the American League, would be to abolish the designated hitter. Reggie Jackson is a designated hitter and a good one, but expensive, isn't he? Don Baylor is a designated hitter and a good one, but he, too, is expensive. Eliminate the DH, and many of them would be replaced by younger, less expensive players.

As I've said before, I regret that Campanella, Reese, Snider, Koufax, Drysdale, Hodges, and others weren't able to make the kind of money players today are getting. They did every bit as much for the game, did they not?

I regret, too, that they won't receive the kind of pension to which the modern player will be entitled. They do nothing to repay the old timers, who in part made it possible for them to earn millions of dollars.

It is disgraceful to see Billy Herman, a Hall of Famer, receiving $3,600 a year on his pension, to see Pee Wee Reese, another Hall of Famer, receiving $7,200 a year on his pension. Some of the players today will receive a $90,000-a-year pension. With the money they earn, they shouldn't need a pension at all.

Gene Autry once went to the Angels' player representative and recommended the players establish a program similar to the one practiced by the members of the Screen Actors Guild. SAG members give one percent of their salaries toward helping the old-timers.

Mr. Autry felt that if players donated one percent of their salaries, baseball's old-timers could then receive an adequate pension. Autry's suggestion fell on deaf ears.

One percent of a player's salary is pocket money these days. A player making $500,000 would donate $5,000, tax deductible. Undoubtedly, he could use the deduction.

I remember when the pension plan was started by the players, who contributed out of their own pockets. It cost them 20 cents a day. Walter O'Malley and George V. McLaughlin, the chairman of the board of the Brooklyn Trust Co., devised the pension plan.

I feel I can talk freely about money, because I never made much from baseball. The most I ever made with the Dodgers was $40,000. In fact, when I was still with the Angels, we had seven players who made more in one year than I made from baseball in my entire career.

Therefore, I can look a player in the eye and say, without reservation, "You're doing the wrong thing. You should take care of the old-timers." It is time the players began giving back to the game that has given them so much. Will it happen? I doubt it.

What the players give back to baseball all too often results in a black eye for the game. Baseball strikes and drug scandals come to mind.

I have no animosity toward the players for striking. It is part of the American way of doing business. They have a right to strike.

My argument is that when the owners got together and decided to go to 24-man rosters, the players collectively cried "collusion." Yet, when the players get together and decide not to play unless their demands are met, it is not collusion. It is a strike. Alas, that is the American way, too.

A question: When Koufax and Drysdale held out together, wasn't that collusion?

On the other matter, I have no sympathy for players who use and abuse drugs. Nor do I have any respect for them. How can you respect a player who makes $600,000 or $800,000 a year but doesn't think enough of his career to stay away from cocaine, a player who would abuse his own body? They have to be idiots.

Cocaine addiction is said to be a disease. I don't buy it. To me, it is a self-inflicted wound. These men had a choice. No one forced them to do the drugs.

In baseball, we deify these fellows, we're hero worshipers. As a result, when they get into trouble, the first thing we do is try to take care of them. We should let them take care of themselves.

When a man in the military service shot himself intentionally to avoid combat, they put a bandage on the wound and sent him to the stockade. When he was healed, they sent him back to the front line. They didn't put him in a $200-a-day rehabilitation center.

Maybe I'm being cold-hearted. But if you're looking for sympathy from me, look elsewhere. I have no sympathy for a man who makes that kind of money and throws it away.

A self-inflicted wound should not entitle a man to sympathy. Why should a drug abuser receive sympathy that I don't get because I don't do drugs?

I was fortunate. In my career, we had just two instances of players involved with drugs, or getting high illegally. Both occurred when I was with the Padres.

The first was a player we got in a trade from Minnesota. We discovered he was getting amphetamines known in baseball as "greenies" from someone in Kansas City, then distributing them to other players. He was making $45,000 with the Padres. I released him outright. He wound up playing in Mexico for $600 a month. Were those greenies worth it?

My son Peter was the general manager of the Padres and Mike Port was the farm director when we signed a young player from the San Diego area to a contract with the Lodi club of the California League. The player was given a $10,000 bonus. Shortly thereafter, he was discovered in his room sniffing glue.

He was immediately given his release, which turned out to be one of the best investments the Padres ever made. Word spread that any such conduct was cause for dismissal. The Padres had no more problems.

In all my years in baseball, I had just three rules, which we administered to all playing personnel before spring training began:

1. Players are not, under any circumstances, to take stimulating drugs of any sort without the express approval of the team physicians. By drugs I mean such stimulants as Dexedrine, amphetamines, Dexyamyl, greenies, uppers, speed, cocaine, heroin, marijuana, or any controlled substance.

2. No player will be permitted in the batting cage without a helmet at any time.

3. I expect all players to respect the flag of the United States during the playing of the National Anthem.

First and foremost was the rule regarding drugs. When I was with the Angels, I had a visit from a gentleman who worked at the CareUnit in Orange.

"Mr. Bavasi," he said, "right now you don't have any players with a problem. But if you ever do, be careful where you send them, which rehab center you send them to."

"Why?" I asked.

"The pushers are smart people. They know where the users are. I can take you to where some of these players go for rehabilitation and the pushers are sitting in the lobby, waiting for the users to come out."

Great.

When Commissioner Peter Ueberroth fined the 11 players in 1986 for their past involvement with drugs, I noticed that not one was with the team for which he played when he was doing drugs. I deduced from this that the teams unloading these players may have suspected a problem, though they did not inform anyone. In a sense, they were unloading damaged goods. Again, where is the integrity?

When the minimum salary was $5,000 instead of $62,000, drugs were not a problem. Before the advent of the Players Association, paternalism ruled, and management could feel free to help players. Today, however, the Association doesn't have the ability to counsel and guide all of its players.

Drugs aren't the only problem. I read about players making unwise investments and losing millions. My advice: if the agent's not available to help, seek help from management. I know the door is still open.

Baseball has not solved its drug problem. As long as there are pushers, there will be users. The drug problem will continue to exist until the government wages and wins a war against drugs being brought into the country.

Two men with whom I was extremely disappointed were Gussie Busch, the owner of the St. Louis Cardinals, and Ted Turner, the owner of the Atlanta Braves. I have always admired both of them, too. I've always liked the way Ted does business. He does not procrastinate. Everything is answered yes or no. He has a lot of courage and he puts his money where his mouth is.

My disappointment in them stems from the same reason: Bowie Kuhn.

We had a meeting in New York regarding Commissioner Kuhn's future. Would he be rehired or not? American League President Lee MacPhail and National League President Chub Feeney decided that each club should voice an opinion about Bowie.

Of the 26 clubs, 21 expressed an interest in retaining Bowie Kuhn. One American League club was against him, four National League clubs were against him.

Two of the four National League clubs, Cincinnati and the New York Mets, gave what they felt were legitimate reasons why Bowie should not be retained. Gussie Busch did not.

"Fire the SOB!" Busch said. I looked over at him and said to myself, "If there's an SOB in this room, it isn't Bowie Kuhn." At that point, I lost respect for Mr. Busch. He would offer no reason whatsoever to have Kuhn fired.

Bowie fined him once, which may have had something to do with Mr. Busch's ill feelings. There was no other clear reason the Cardinals could have been opposed to rehiring Bowie Kuhn as commissioner.

I might have understood his resentment had he owned a superstation like Ted Turner's WTBS. Bowie was opposed to superstations' televising baseball games, because he felt they might affect other clubs' and baseball's network television contracts. But Gussie doesn't own a superstation.

Ted Turner had good reason to go along with Gussie. One, Turner had his own superstation. Two, Anheuser-Busch was a major sponsor on WTBS.

Before we got to the meeting, Bowie had negotiated an impressive television package with the networks. It was easily the best package we'd ever had. Ted Turner was extensively quoted in the paper, "This is such a great contract, I'm changing my mind about voting against Bowie Kuhn."

At the meeting, Ted stood up and put the rap on Bowie and the plan. I wouldn't listen. I stood up, with the newspaper clipping in my hand, and spoke.

"It states here that somebody in this room is saying this is such a good package 'I think I'll change my mind and vote for the commissioner.' Do you know who said that, Mr. Turner? You did."

He started to mumble something, but sat down. I'll say this for him. He did not vote against the television package: he passed. As a result, I still have a lot of respect for him.

However, if he had kept his word and voted for Bowie's re-election, Bowie Kuhn would still be the commissioner.

This should not be construed to reflect on Peter Ueberroth and the job he's done. I think he has done a remarkable job. He has the power that he needs. He is independent. He doesn't need this job, which is important. I like the way he's done business.

But I also think Bowie would have done the same things if he had the authority Peter Ueberroth was given when he assumed control.

It is possible that in five or six years, clubs won't have to draw two million or more fans simply to break even. Maybe 1.5 million fans will be the break-even point for some of the clubs, and all because of some of the things Peter has put into effect already.

Going to 24-man rosters is a step in the right direction. I've been with clubs that won pennants with 23-man rosters. By dropping the 25th man, the club increases the value of utility players, men who can play more than one position, and in the process saves the club money.

When we made a first baseman out of Frank Howard, who was 6'7", he was irate. "You're only doing it to take advantage of my height," he said.

"That's right," I said. "You're absolutely right. But, Frank, take Gil Hodges. Hodges could play third base, first base, and catcher. Junior Gilliam can play every infield position except shortstop and he can play the outfield."

The more positions you can play, the more valuable you are to a club, particularly a club carrying just 24 players.

I am also disillusioned with the way Hall of Fame selections are made. I've come to understand why we have the Veterans Committee, of which I am a member: to correct the mistakes made by the baseball writers who vote.

Enos Slaughter, for instance, had the same kinds of records as did Jackie Robinson, except Enos did it for 15 years instead of 10. It took a vote of the Veterans Committee to get Slaughter into the Hall of Fame.

A lot of writers apparently think they have to list 10 players on their ballots. They don't. Darold Knowles, for example, got four votes one year. With all due respect to Darold, he doesn't deserve to be mentioned in the same breath as the Hall of Fame.

When I see some of the names eligible, I nearly get sick to my stomach. Why are they even mentioned? And then you see that Roger Maris fails to get elected, you begin to wonder about the election process.

One criterion says a player cannot be elected to the Hall of Fame simply for setting one record. The fact that Maris hit 61 home runs in 1961 in itself is not enough to warrant his election.

However, Maris was the American League's Most Valuable Player two years in a row, as well as the record-holder for most home runs in a season. How many other players were ever so honored with two

MVP awards? I wonder if the reason Maris is not in the Hall of Fame is that some people aren't aware that he was a two-time MVP.

The Hall of Fame is becoming a popularity contest. Players who were rude to the press or, like Steve Carlton, did not speak with the press, likely will be left off some Hall of Fame ballots.

There is no doubt in my mind that four years from now, Rod Carew will deserve to be elected into the Hall of Fame. Unfortunately, he was not diplomatic with the press, and it may cost him a first-ballot election.

Baseball has so many things wrong with it today. A man making $900,000 a year insists on a single hotel room on the road, at the club's expense. For $900,000 a year, you'd think the player would pay for it himself.

Players complain about each other far more today than they ever did. In my later years, I had players come into the office and say, "Can't you talk to so and so about this or that?" I wasn't used to that.

In the era of the train, players lived with each other, they ate meals together, they shared rooms, they knew each other.

The airplane and lucrative contracts have made virtual strangers of men who spend seven months a year together. It's sad.

The game itself has not changed. The people have changed, the attitudes have changed. Players are not motivated by winning anymore. They're motivated by money.

Alas, baseball is a prisoner of money. In the last two decades, dollars have replaced sense.

19

A Trade I Wouldn't Make

When I announced my retirement in August of 1984, I received the following telegram:

Dear Buzzie,
Say it ain't so! There's no rule that says just because the commissioner goes, his friends have to go, too. Whatever you do, you have my friendship and esteem and the affection of all the Kuhn family.

Best always,
Bowie

At one time, I was foolish enough to think that baseball was my life. I was sure I would die with my boots on. In the end, it was only my career. I no longer enjoyed it the way it was meant to be enjoyed.

So I retired. What I immediately discovered was that the game was fun for me again. The magic had returned. I found I enjoyed watching and listening to games. I could watch a game on television, second-guess a manager, criticize a player, turn the television set off, and forget about it. The problems were no longer mine.

Since I've retired, I watch baseball differently. I watch it to be entertained. I am a fan again. I still like to see the Dodgers, the Angels, and the Padres do well, but if they don't, it is not my concern.

Evit says she won't allow me to get a satellite dish because it would be an eyesore. In reality, she doesn't want me watching any more games than I already watch. Now, I watch and listen to more baseball games than I ever have. I'll often have two television sets and a radio working simultaneously.

My day begins with the morning newspapers. I read the sports pages, then do the crossword puzzles. I turn on "The Price is Right" with Bob Barker, a show I enjoy, probably because in my latter years in baseball, the price was never right.

I go down to La Jolla Cove and take pictures of the seals there. I return home and settle in for a day of baseball. I'm fortunate to be in La Jolla, where our radio and television reception comes from both Los Angeles and San Diego. I can follow the Dodgers, Angels, and Padres.

Usually, one team will be playing in the East, which means its games come on earlier. The only time I have problems is when the Padres are at San Francisco, the Dodgers are home, and the Angels are in Seattle all at the same time. It's tough to wear two ear plugs at once.

Evit, I'm sure, is starting to wonder. One day she was ready to call Vin Scully, to chew him out: Evit likes to watch M*A*S*H at 7:30, but the Dodger post-game show was running overtime on the same channel.

I do miss certain aspects of the game. I miss the

association with the old-timers, people who have been in the game a long time, men like Jim Campbell, Haywood Sullivan, Gabe Paul, Bing Devine, and other general managers.

I miss the stories that baseball provided us. I was reminded of one involving a tryout camp we held in Thomasville, North Carolina in 1941, run by Fresco Thompson. Larry MacPhail, the president of the Dodgers, was sitting in the stands watching the workout.

"Who the hell is that fat kid there?" Larry asked, pointing to a portly player. Fresco said it was some youngster who came in for a tryout.

"He looks like he's a pretty good player," Fresco said. "We might sign him."

"No, you're not," Larry said. "Get him out of camp."

Eight years later, the fat kid we ran out of camp led the American League in hitting. His name was George Kell.

I miss the association with some of the players, although at the end it wasn't the same. Players now have other matters with which to concern themselves. Most of them no longer have time to come into the office to talk baseball. I miss going to the baseball meetings. I miss visiting the other cities.

But I do not miss the business aspect of the game at all. I had grown so disgruntled with the way the game was being operated; it had ceased to be fun. It had become a job. And to me, baseball was not meant to be work.

Thus, the time had come for me to move on and to leave the game in the hands of younger men. It was time for me to get back to enjoying both life and baseball. And I have. Evit and I are traveling extensively, seeing parts of the country and the world that we previously had been unable to see.

So far, we've cruised through the Panama Canal and to Alaska, and traveled cross-country by train. We've driven to several national parks and nearly every state. We've seen Niagara falls and Mt. Rushmore and innumerable other wonderful places. For the first time in our lives, we've had summer vacations.

No one in baseball took summer vacations until the new breed took over. Incredibly, there are now those who work in baseball and take vacations during the season. I find this ridiculous. We worked hard, winter or summer, because we loved it. Spring training, two months in Florida, was vacation enough.

Appropriately, spring training in Florida was the first trip Evit and I took upon retiring. We went back in time, really, for the 30th reunion of the 1955 Brooklyn Dodgers in Vero Beach, to honor the club's first world championship team.

Campy was there. So were Pee Wee, Billy Loes, Carl Furillo, Roger Craig, Eddie Roebuck, Joe Black, Don Newcombe, Carl Erskine, Bob Borkowski, Sandy Amoros. Everyone was there except Don Zimmer, who was opening spring training in Arizona with the Cubs, and Duke Snider, who had a broadcasting commitment with the Expos.

Some of them did not look much different than they did 30 years ago. It was a great team. These men knew how to play the game.

One year earlier, Pee Wee Reese had been selected to the Hall of Fame by the Veterans Committee, of which I was a member. The roads inside Dodgertown are all named after Dodgers in the Hall of Fame, and while we were there, they named one for Pee Wee.

"Pee Wee," I said facetiously, "this is a big honor. But if you remember, years ago, this road led straight out to a house of ill repute."

It looked like it still could—it was not yet paved. In

his acceptance speech, Pee Wee asked Peter O'Malley if they could at least pave the road.

That '55 club was a special club, and seeing it together again was a wonderful way to begin our retirement.

I left the game with few regrets. One regret, though, was that we could not win a pennant for Gene Autry. Otherwise, I can say I had a career I would not trade for any other. I suppose if I could turn the clock back 50 years, I'd still go into baseball.

I'm very happy with the way my life turned out. I have four fine sons and five wonderful grandchildren. I've had a career that left me with memories that will last a lifetime.

Another story:

Walter O'Malley's daughter, Terry, was about 12 years old, and she was watching a Dodgers-St. Louis game. Fred Saigh, the owner of the Cardinals, was nearby. He had been indicted and he was going to prison.

"Oh, Mr. Saigh, I didn't know you had a boat," she said to him.

"What do you mean, young lady?"

"Somebody said you were going up the river."

The innocence of youth is a wonderful thing.

A couple of years ago, the innocence of youth was demonstrated by a young outfielder in the Angels' organization, Devon White. Thinking he was turning on the air conditioning of the team bus, which was parked, he inadvertently started the bus, and ran it into a wall. He insisted on paying for all the damage himself.

The Angels would not allow him to pay for it but just the fact he made the offer impressed me. The innocence of youth. Here was a young man who took responsibility for his own actions.

With young men like this in the game, it leads me to believe there is still hope for baseball.

On the day my retirement was announced in the newspapers, another story caught my attention. It was regarding Black's Beach, a notorious nude beach that was not beyond the range of my telescope. The story announced the city was banning nude sunbathing there.

Now that I would finally be spending my summers at home, they had taken away my view.